FIRST STEPS IN RAILWAY MODELLING

C. J. FREEZER

Midland Publishing

CONTENTS

First Steps in Railway Modelling
© Cyril J. Freezer 1998

ISBN 1 85780 066 4

Published in 1998 by Midland Publishing,
24 The Hollow, Earl Shilton,
Leicester LE9 7NA, England
Tel: 01455 847 815   Fax: 01455 841 805
E-mail: midlandbooks@compuserve.com

Design, concept and layout
© 1998 Midland Publishing and
Stephen Thompson Associates.

Reprinted 2000 in England by Ian Allan Printing Ltd, Riverdene Business Park, Hersham, KT12 4RG.

Midland Publishing is an imprint of Ian Allan Publishing Ltd.

Midland Publishing gratefully acknowledges the help of David Brown of *British Railway Modelling* magazine for the use of several photos in this book.

Our associate company stocks a huge selection of railway and railway modelling books and videos, for worldwide mail order. See their adverts in the popular modelling press or write for the latest free catalogues to Midland Counties Publications, 4 Watling Drive, Hinckley, Leics, LE10 3EY (telephone 01455 254 450)

Front cover photographs:

Main picture: **LNER J72 8680, a Bachmann Branch-line 0-6-0 tank engine, crosses the road bridge on Alan Wright's 'Ingle Nook Sidings'.**

Lower left: **English Electric Type 1, later Class 20, D8046 at 'Melbridge Dock', a minimum space 4mm scale layout.** Photograph by Tony Wright

Lower right: **DMU Class 158 enters Knowle Bridge station on Sheffield Model Railway Enthusiasts N gauge 'Edgedale & Nether Gill' layout.** Photograph by Tony Wright

INTRODUCTION

The growth of commercial support over recent years now makes it possible to enjoy railway modelling without having first to construct every item from basic components. Nevertheless there are some parts of a layout that are more conveniently made in the home, tailored to your own requirements. In this book I will show how you can create small, interesting layouts using techniques that have been tried and tested through the years. Furthermore the tools and materials required can easily be found in any moderately large town. Alas not all changes have made life easier. The reaction to solvent abuse and knife attacks has led to youngsters being denied the ability to purchase for themselves two essential tools of the craft, plastic adhesives and craft knives, and so parental help must be sought at the very outset.

As the title of this book implies, I am dealing with the *basics* of the hobby, covering sufficient ground to allow a newcomer to create a convincing model railway that can be operated in a railwaylike manner. Inevitably many advanced topics and techniques have either been totally ignored or, at best, mentioned briefly. Experienced critics should bear this in mind, diving in the deep end is not the most sensible way of learning to swim.

Since it is my belief that, in the early stages of the hobby, ready availability is the most important factor in the choice of products, I have concentrated on the most widely available size, 00 gauge. This in no way infers that other sizes are in any way inferior, it's just that many excellent choices are not that easy to find, while other worthy options are effectively ruled out unless you not only possess a well-equipped workshop, but can handle a wide range of specialised tools. That almost anyone can acquire the necessary skills if they are determined enough to practice the craft is immaterial: this takes time and considerable dedication. At the outset you need to get something up and running as quickly as possible whilst enthusiasm is at white heat. Once that is done, you can elaborate to your heart's content. And, believe me, there is nothing, absolutely nothing, that lends itself better to elaboration than a model railway.

C.J. Freezer
Hemel Hempstead, 1998

DIMENSIONS

Although Britain is supposed to have converted to metric standards, not only do many of us continue to think in feet and inches, but imperial standards are still widely used in day to day business. The survival of the foot and inch derives from the fact that, except where precision is important, they are more convenient units than the approved metric figures of metre and millimetre. Therefore, the dimensions of baseboards and rooms are given in imperial standards.

However, the value of the millimetre for modelmaking is undeniable, it has been used in railway modelling since the mid-1930s. When you go into the majority of DIY outlets to buy timber and man-made boards (ply, chipboard, MDF and hardboard) you will find dimensions given in millimetres, hence I have quoted these sized in metric, with imperial equivalents in brackets.

Similarly bolts and nuts are only available in metric sizes, but woodscrews are still described by their old gauge diameter with their length in inches.

This is only confusing if you believe that you should not use two systems of measurement at once. This is a fallacy, the only time you do need to observe unity is when you are making calculations. You can however cut a piece of wood three feet long and mark the position of a cross piece 19mm in from one end, using the same rule to make your marks.

Equivalent sizes are calculated on the basis of the 'metric inch' or 25mm and the 'metric foot' of 300mm rather than the 'more correct' figures of 25.4mm and 304.8mm respectively, for the simple reason that it is essential to work in round figures when one is using a rule for marking out. Your limit of accuracy is determined by the scale division. When I specify a drill, I have given the sizes of available tool bits.

Title page photograph:
'Oxendale Junction', part of an N gauge layout built by the Wolverhampton Model Railway Club, set on the British Railways Western Region, during the transitional steam to diesel era. An example of the type of layout that you can eventually progress to if you begin by following the techniques outlined in this book. Photograph by Tony Wright

GLOSSARY

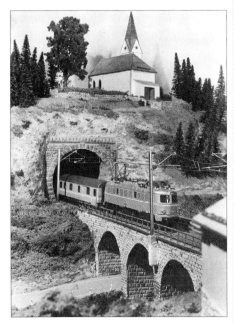

Top: **4mm scale GWR Prairie on Phillip George's 'Coedway' layout.** Photograph by Tony Wright courtesy of *Model Railways*

Centre: **A 4mm scale Lima parcels diesel railcar modified, re-wheeled and re-painted to BR Western Region livery.** Photograph by Tony Wright

Bottom: **European HO on Howard and Eileen Lawrence's 'Saafeld am See'.** Photograph by Tony Wright, courtesy of *Continental Modeller* magazine

AC Alternating current. Electric current which changes polarity in a regular cycle. It is the normal mains supply.

Advanced uncoupling A system of automatic uncoupling where the vehicles are pushed over an actuating mechanism which uncouples them, leaving the vehicles uncoupled whilst being pushed.

Auto-coupler A device for automatically coupling locomotives and rolling stock when pushed together. Frequently, the vehicles can also be uncoupled, normally at a ramp or magnet situated in the track.

Baseboard The substructure on which a model railway is built.

Baseboard unit One part of a sectional layout.

Bracket signal A semaphore signal array with two or more arms indicating different routes ahead. Found at junctions and station approaches where there is more than one platform or running road. Often termed junction signal.

Bridge rectifier An arrangement of four diodes which converts both cycles of an AC input to DC. Additional smoothing devices are required for pure DC but the unsmoothed output is adequate for most model railway purposes.

Broad gauge Any railway with a gauge wider than 4ft 8½in. Often regarded solely as applying to Brunel's defunct 7ft gauge, it also applies to contemporary Irish, Iberian, Russian, Indian and some Australian railways.

Controller A device that modifies a 12 volt DC supply to control speed and direction of a locomotive.

Bridge rail This form of flat based rail was formerly used on the broad gauge GWR. The Broad Gauge Society have had sections drawn for 4 and 7mm scales.

Bullhead rail A pattern of rail used mainly in Great Britain until 1950. It has a narrow base and is secured to the sleeper with chairs. It is still in use, particularly on the London Underground system. On model railways it is mainly found on accurate steam age models.

Cassette A specialised form of fiddle yard. The trains run onto a length of track, usually made from inverted aluminium angle. Complete trains can be juggled in this fashion.

Catenary The complex arrangement of contact and support wires of an electrified railway is a catenary. This term is often loosely applied to the entire overhead.

Centre third A system of current collection using a central third rail. Formerly used by ready-to-run systems and now virtually obsolete.

Command control A system of model railway control where a constant voltage is applied to the rails. Each locomotive or railcar is fitted with a decoder which interprets a command sent over the rails. The control unit incorporates advanced electronics and requires a microprocessor. It permits independent operation of two or more trains in the same section of track, which is not an unalloyed blessing since this can (and usually does) lead to collisions. It also eliminates most wiring which is a great benefit on very large layouts. It also has its value on very simple systems, and, for the railway modeller who uses sectional track to make frequent modifications to the layout, it is a sheer necessity. To borrow a term from computing, it gives plug and play operation. Against this, the cost of the central unit is very high and modules not only add to the cost of each locomotive, they need to be fitted. The system got off to a very bad start in Britain, with two incompatible systems introduced simultaneously, one of which was quickly dropped, the other was not developed or supported. The US based NMRA (qv) has established a set of standards and recent British command control systems conform to these rules. However, for a medium sized British layout, the hard wired system is more cost effective.

Computer control Various attempts to control model railways by computer have been tried. There are many problems, not the least of which is that a computer keyboard is not exactly the ideal device to control a model railway. The easiest solution is to eliminate the models and simulate the railway workings on the monitor. Such programs are readily available. You have the option of simulating the workings of modern centralised control over actual sections of railway, or of designing your dream layout, without consideration of size or cost, and then running trains over the tracks. So far we have not a true multimedia train driving simulation, but modern home computers have this capacity. In other words, virtual railway modelling is wholly practical and takes up very little actual space.

Crossing 1) A track formation that crosses one track over another without any connection, as at a double junction. Frequently termed a diamond crossing. 2) In strict railway parlance, the part of a turnout where the rails cross.

Culvert A small bridge or large drain carrying a stream under a railway.

Cutting A large trench with sloping walls and railway tracks at the bottom.

DC Direct current. Electric current of constant polarity as supplied by batteries or from AC supplies via a rectifier.

Diesel Era A more accurate term for Modern Image (qv)

Diode An electronic device that will only pass DC current in one direction. It will produce a pulsating DC output from AC by suppressing one half of each cycle.

Gauge The distance between the inner faces of the rails.

Distant signal A warning signal, normally ¼ mile in front of a home signal giving the driver time to slow down and stop.

Embankment A bank of soil to carry a railway line (or other track) above the natural ground level.

Epoch As in Britain, German railway modellers and manufacturers exploit the nostalgic value of the steam age. Whereas in Britain the various eras are given descriptive names, the Germans broke their timescale into Epochs, possibly because they were reluctant to give a name to the very innovative 1930s. Unfortunately, not only does the Epoch system require a crib sheet, but, being based sensibly on the obvious design breaks, when applied to other systems, ie, the Swiss, the dates had to be changed. With hindsight the decade system which is slowly gaining currency, would be better.

Exhibition circuit When a model railway is invited to more than one exhibition within a year, it has entered the exhibition circuit. Its owner is then liable to find his spare time bespoke and needs to collect a small band of helpers to man the layout and help move and erect it. In extreme cases, the layout may only be operated at exhibitions, being too large to fully assemble in its home base. This is very advanced railway modelling.

Fiddle yard A series of offstage storage tracks used to hold trains so they can emerge in turn on the layout proper, ideally to a schedule. It is permissible to rearrange the train formation in a fiddle yard.

Finescale A contradiction in terms, since the scale is not affected. Originally applied to a more accurate system of track and wheels for 0 gauge, it has become to mean models are built to more exacting standards of detail and accuracy than current commercial products. It usually means what the speaker intends it to mean, neither more nor less.

Flanges The projection on a railway wheel which keeps them on the track.

Flat bottom rail As the name implies, this section rail has a wide flat base. It was formerly called Vignoles rail.

Flatbottom rail The standard rail section in use on all modern systems. The rail has a wide base and, originally, was spiked directly to the sleeper. With increasing train loadings, baseplates were introduced to spread the load and on all but lightly laid track now has the rail secured either by bolts and clips or patent clips.

Frog The part of a turnout where the inner rails cross. In strict railway parlance, this is a crossing.

Gantry signal A light-weight bridge structure crossing several tracks carrying many signal posts or colour light heads. Only found at large stations or over quadruple tracks in confined sites. Often used on a model to a) fit in three or more signals in the usually confined space on the model and b) to create the illusion that the station is an important one.

Gradient The slope of a railway. It can be expressed as a percentage (%), as per mile (⁰/₀₀) or, more commonly in Britain, as a ratio (1 in xxx). The ratio is easier to use in railway modelling, a 1 in 40 grade means a rise of one unit every forty units of measurement (inches, feet, millimetres, centimetres or metres). The important point to remember is that the higher the ratio the shallower the grade, whereas the higher the percentage, the steeper the grade.

Home signal The semaphore signal controlling entry into a block section.

Interurban An American term used to describe light railway systems (almost invariably electrified) which link nearby towns (inter-urban = between towns). In town centres the lines usually run along streets, but in the country they are either beside the highway or strike across country.

Level crossing A road crossing on the level. Formerly closed by gates, but today lifting barriers are preferred.

Light railway Legally, a light railway is a railway authorised under the Light Railway Act by means of an Order issued by the Department of Transport rather than an enabling Act. Such lines were frequently built to less exacting standards and, according to the individual Order, could omit certain features required on normal railways (eg, raised platforms, complete fencing, etc). Most preserved railways operate under a Light Railway Order, but are otherwise indistinguishable from a 'proper railway'.

Livery The paint scheme for a locomotive or coach.

Modern image A term introduced in the 1960s to describe the then new diesel hauled and (occasionally) electrified trains on British Rail. The object was to distinguish between current practice and the historic steam hauled system. With the rapid development of new train designs and the simplification of track layouts, it is now necessary to distinguish between current practice and 'Historic Modern Image.'

Multiple aspect Modern colour light signals have three or four aspects, ie arrangements of lights. Green indicates line ahead clear, red indicates line ahead blocked (ie, occupied by another train). A single yellow light indicates that the signal ahead is showing red, two yellow lights (double yellow) indicates that the signal ahead is yellow.

Narrow gauge Any prototype railway with a gauge less than 4ft 8½in is 'narrow' gauge. Such railways fall into two groups, relatively short feeder systems, usually associated with mineral traffic (eg, the Festiniog Railway) and major systems which are either situated in mountainous regions (eg, the several Swiss metre gauge systems) or, in the case of 3ft 6in, metre or 3ft gauge, are the *de facto* standard gauge for certain countries (eg, New Zealand's 3ft 6in systems). Narrow gauge modelling is now well established.

NEM The Continental European equivalent of the NMRA. Less effective than the American body, since the larger manufacturers do what they were going to do anyway.

NMRA National Model Railway Association. An American organisation that, among other things, sets standards for fundamental features of model railways. Their wheel standards for 16.5mm gauge are slowly gaining international acceptance.

Occupation bridge A small underbridge maintaining access between parts of an estate or farm bisected by a railway embankment or cutting.

Occupation crossing A level crossing provided to maintain access between parts of an estate or farm bisected by a railway. It is more correctly an uncontrolled crossing, since no warning of a train's approach is given to users.

Overbridge A bridge carrying a road or canal over a railway.

Overhead supply Most prototype electrified railways have an overhead feed, the rails forming the return. Models of modern electrified railways should be so equipped, but in most instances the overhead is only a cosmetic feature.

Some ready-to-run models are fitted with a changeover switch permitting the model to collect from the overhead wire.

Point 1) A track formation where two tracks are linked to one that allows trains to be diverted to one of two tracks. Also known as turnout. 2) In strict railway parlance, the tapered rails of a point. Generally used in the plural.

Portable layout A model railway which can be easily moved from place to place. Increasingly applied to layouts that are normally stored in a dismantled form and only erected for operating sessions. See transportable layout.

Pre-group In 1922, the many independent companies that formed Britain's railway system were compulsorily amalgamated into four groups. Any model set prior to this date is pre-group. The term is going out of use as historical railway modelling becomes more diverse.

Private owner A wagon or van owned by a company or trading partnership for exclusive use by the owner.

Prototype The full size original on which a model is based.

Rapid transit An urban railway which is characterised by a very frequent service of trains but which have a low overall speed since frequent station stops are made. The London Underground is the best-known British rapid transit system.

Rectifier An electronic device which converts AC current to DC.

Relay An electro-magnetic switch which is employed to change circuits.

R to R Abbreviation for 'ready to run' – in connection with commercially produced locomotives and rolling stock, for use 'straight from the box'.

Scale The ratio between sizes on the prototype and model, expressed either as a ratio (1:76, 1/76 or 1 to 76) or linear equivalent (4mm to 1 foot).

Signal box A structure housing a lever frame controlling points and signals on a section of track. Early systems were wholly mechanical and only controlled a limited area. Modern electro-mechanical installations control large sections of a railway, the signalmen rely on illuminated panels and monitors to track the position of trains.

Steam age A useful portmanteau term used to knit together all model railways set in a period prior to dieselisation.

Stud contact A system of current collection where the feed is through a series of studs along the centre line of the track. Locomotives are fitted with a long skate. Used by Märklin for their non-standard HO system and by many garden railway workers in 0 and 1 gauges.

Three-rail A system of electrical supply where the rails form the return and a third rail forms the feed. It is now obsolete with models, but still used on the electrified lines of the

former Southern region and on London Underground and other rapid transit systems. Models based on these systems usually use two-rail supply with cosmetic third (and fourth) rails.

Track 1) An assembly of two rails set at a fixed gauge held in fixings to a series of wooden cross beams termed sleepers. 2) A loose description of a series of tracks forming a layout.

Train turntable A form of fiddle yard where the entire yard turns around a central pivot. It is mainly used on exhibition oriented layouts since, in the home, there is rarely room to swing the table.

Tramway overhead Electric trams collect current from a single contact wire. A few small electrified railways and interurban lines also use a single wire. It shows considerable economy, but is only suitable for low speed operation.

Tramway Originally used to describe early mineral horse-worked systems, the term is now always applied to electric street level rail systems.

Transformer A device to change the line voltage of an electric current. It will only work with AC supplies.

Transportable layout A model railway that is normally erected, but being built on several baseboard units, can be dismantled and taken to another site, generally a public exhibition.

Traverser A mechanical arrangement whereby a track, or series of tracks can be moved sideways to line up with other fixed tracks. On the prototype it is generally used in repair works, and, in Continental Europe, in modern electric or diesel locomotive depots. Commercial versions are available. In British modelling it is usually used as for fiddle yards.

Turnout A track formation where two tracks are linked to one. More commonly termed point.

Two aspect A colour light signal with just two lights, red/green or red/yellow. It is a straight replacement of a semaphore signal.

Two-rail The common system of current collection on model railways, where the rails are insulated one from another and the current fed to each rail. All wheels must be insulated.

Underbridge A railway bridge spanning a road or waterway.

Below: **A 4mm scale GWR 14xx 0-4-2T, hauling an horse box and a 'B' coach set, on Phillip George's 'Coedway' layout.** Photograph by Tony Wright

CHAPTER 1

MAKING A START!

When I first took a serious interest in railway modelling, it was easy to distinguish between a proper model railway and a well-developed train set. One had only to look at the track, the train set ran on tinplate track, with very deep round-topped flat bottom rail clenched into tinplate pod sleepers, whereas the model railway had proper permanent way with solid drawn bullhead section rail held in whitemetal chairs which were pinned to wooden sleepers, just like the real thing. Furthermore, the train set had lithographed tinplate locomotives, coaches and wagons, while the model railway had stock built from metal or wood. To the more experienced eye, it was clear that the model railway's locomotives, coaches and wagons were closely patterned on actual full sized machines whereas most of the toys were at best, caricatures of their supposed originals.

Today there are gaudy plastic toy trains intended for the under eight market, which we can ignore. There are the affordable mass-produced ready-to-run systems which, while sold by the better toy retailers, are in every respect, more accurate models of their prototypes than the best pre-war 'super detail scale models' which were priced far outside the pockets of most enthusiasts. The track is identical to the basic track supplied for the scale market and the products are also sold In model shops and are used by most committed railway modellers. The distinction between toy train set and model railway appears to have vanished.

In fact it remains where it was at the turn of the century. Back in the early days of the hobby, there were men who took the best available tinplate models and created from sectional tinplate track, miniature systems that could be worked in a prototypical fashion. The line probably began at a three-platform 'Euston' from which a short length of double track brought one to 'Crewe', where the 'Holyhead' branch peeled off and a single track ran on to a terminus at 'Carlisle'. By current standards, it was crude in the extreme but one could run a loose facsimile of the old LNWR timetable. The model 'Irish Mail' or 'Corridor' started and ended at their proper places. This was, and remains the essential difference. A model railway can be operated according to prototype practice, one can only play trains on a developed train set.

We will go further into this in a later chapter. We will also explore the construction of the infrastructure of the model in some detail. For the moment we need to consider the three elements of the model which will be bought in a ready to run state, the power supply, the track and the locomotives and rolling stock.

Power supplies, like any mains powered be idiot proof, modern model railway power supplies are tamper resistant and internally protected so provided you don't try to open the casing, switch on if the casing is wet, use it if the lead is damaged or, worst of all, cut the plug off the lead in order to lengthen it, you have no worries. Well, you do have one small problem, the standard 2 metre lead is almost always too short to reach the wall socket. The simple answer is to buy an extension lead.

The sectional track used in train sets by Hornby and Lima is perfectly suitable at the outset, but for serious work you may well wish to use flexible track and larger radius turnouts (points). The best known make is Peco, this British product is rated as the most reliable system in the world. All these tracks conform to the same standards, with a track gauge of 16.5mm and Code 100 rail in plastic sleepers. The code number gives the height of the rail in thousandths of an inch. This track, usually referred to as 00/HO, is an accepted international standard and is the one best suited for newcomers.

We all start this way, with a train set laid out on the floor, taking up a lot of room. It has to be laboriously put together before running can begin, then packed away at the end, hopefully in a neat and orderly manner. All the while it is at risk of being trodden upon. There has to be a better way. There is, as we shall see in this book.

equipment, must conform to rigorous safety standards. They should be purchased from a reputable dealer rather than from an unknown source. Once the potentially lethal mains voltage has been reduced in the unit to the safe low voltages needed to power the model, you can play around with the wiring in complete safety. While no mains powered equipment can

Finally, we come to the locomotives, coaches and wagons. In the past twenty years the situation has changed dramatically, we are now faced with so wide a choice that even an experienced railway modeller has difficulty deciding which next to buy. The newcomer can be excused for feeling it is all too difficult. This is exacerbated by the old outdated advice to select

Above: **Eastern region J72 0-6-0 *Joem*, an attractive example of a small steam age shunting loco, made by Mainline, is ideally suited for initial testing, yet has considerable value when the layout reaches operational condition.**

Below: **A Bachmann ready-to-run British Railways diesel mechanical 04 shunter; another good testing loco which will have further use as the layout develops. Although most of the prototype BR machines have been scrapped some were sold to industrial users and preservation societies.**

a prototype and period before you begin to collect your locomotive stud. This is unnecessary.

It will take some time to build the baseboards, lay the track and connect it to the power unit through a control panel. You will then be involved with landscaping and adding the various lineside buildings and platforms. During this time, all you need is a 'works train'. A small six-coupled shunting locomotive, either steam or diesel outline, a couple of coaches and a small assortment of wagons is perfectly adequate for this. Don't worry about the prototype, this initial collection should be looked on as expendable. Long experience shows that not only do most newcomers change their ideas in the first year, but, more to the point, most of the 'works train' will take a dive from the baseboard to the floor sometime during construction. It needs to be expendable.

So far I've said nothing about scale and only, by implication, mentioned gauge. On paper, there is a wide choice of scale/gauge combinations. One can spend days agonising over which is best since almost everyone looks at this from the obvious aspect of technical excellence. Unfortunately, most of the factors that need to be considered are conditional, the question is really 'best for what purpose?' You will meet many railway modellers committed to a particular scale/gauge combination who will happily spend hours extolling the virtues and advantages of their choice. Very rarely will you meet anyone ready to point out the disadvantages - and there is no approach to the hobby which does not have its down side.

There are however two factors that are absolute. The first is cost, an important

consideration for the beginner who, by definition, starts with a clean sheet. Although, in the long run, differential costs tend to even out between the scales and gauges, in the short term they are very significant.

Even more significant at the outset is availability. You need to know that the essential equipment for your layout can not only be bought locally but that there will be reasonable supplies in the shop. There is nothing more frustrating than to discover that not only have you run out of an essential item, but that your local dealer hasn't any on his shelves.

There is, at the time of writing, only one size that meets both requirements – 00 gauge, 4mm scale on 16.5mm gauge. For this reason, the three layout designs I am discussing are based on this size, though the principles involved are common to all scales. While it is not a case of 00 first and the rest nowhere, it is, at the time of writing, still the size you are most likely to find on sale in the High Street. Indeed, there are many well established railway modellers who rarely, if ever, buy their requirements anywhere else and a surprisingly large number who are unaware that there are other products they could use to advantage.

This uninformed group have one thing in common, they never read model railway magazines. There is no excuse for this, the larger newsagents devote a reasonable amount of space to model and prototype railway magazines. Magazines not only tell you about other enthusiast's layouts and show you how to tackle modelling projects, they provide a wealth of information on the products available, the firms who make and sell them and the exhibitions and swapmeets that take place almost every weekend of the year. The most comprehensive exhibition listings are to be found in *Railway Modeller*, which also has the largest advertising section of any British magazine. Magazines are essential if you wish to get anywhere in the hobby.

It is also a good idea to visit your local model railway exhibition and, if possible, one of the larger shows. Not only will you see numerous layouts, you will also have the opportunity of seeing a wide selection of products on the trade stands. The local shows, while on a smaller scale, usually include a club sales stand, where you can find the odd bargain, and, more to the point, are supported by local model shops. Most important of all, you can meet fellow enthusiasts.

Reading magazines and visiting exhibitions will show you many different approaches to the hobby. All are equally valid and it would be very unusual were you not to wonder if a different approach to the one you began with might not be better for you. Whether you do anything about it is another matter. It is always possible to make out a good case for modelling any prototype at any point in time to any scale. It is less obvious that the finest design on paper is vastly inferior to an actual working model railway. The harsh reality is that limitations of space, money and modelling time have a very strong influence on how far short of the ideal the layout will fall.

The important thing at the outset is to get something up and running as quickly as possible. Once you've done that, you can start thinking about refinements. In all probability you will rapidly move on to building a completely different layout, for very few established railway modellers

Above: **Attention to detail creates realism. The bicycle leaning against the concrete platelayer's hut adds life to this scene, but the most telling touch is the prototypical alignment of the post and wire boundary fence.**

Centre left: **Two Ratio kits were the foundation of this little scene. The signal box was made up according to the instructions, since the kit was appropriate for its purpose. The grounded coach body has been extensively 'distressed' to create** the impression of dilapidation such structures acquired over time. The far side is in even worse condition!

Centre right: **Steam locomotives required huge quantities of water and so water cranes were a commonplace fitting before the advent of diesel and electric traction. In the foreground the edge of another steam age feature, the inspection pit, which allowed easier access to the internal mechanism of the steam locomotive can be seen.**

end up with something bearing the slightest resemblance to the one they first built. Changing your mind is all part of the fun, but you cannot begin to make an informed choice without considerable experience and you only gain experience by building a layout.

As with the works train, it's a good idea to look on the initial layout as expendable.

Right: **Part-complete landscaping on an N gauge Continental model. Here advantage has been taken of the ability to negotiate small radii to loop the tracks back on themselves, with the sharp curves hidden in tunnel.**

CHAPTER 2

BASEBOARD BASICS

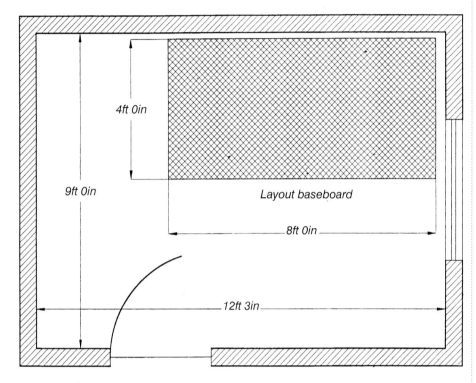

Figure 2/1

Figure 2/2

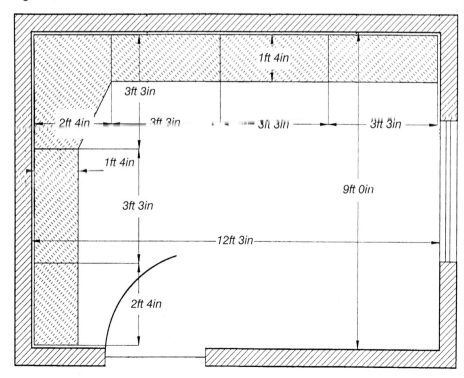

The first step forward from the simple train set, laid out afresh before each running session, then put neatly away in its boxes (or merely piled into a large carton to save time) is to fix the tracks onto a raised baseboard. This saves the bother of setting them out each time and allows the wiring to be fixed in place as well. Most of all, scenic development can only take place on a baseboard.

Laying tracks onto a baseboard does not necessarily produce a model railway. The usual beginner's idea, an oval of track with sidings, is no more than a developed train set. The only running that can take place is simple tail chasing around the oval. Good fun though this can be at the start, it soon palls. Since lack of operating challenge is the commonest cause of loss of interest, we need to create a layout which allows us to run our small trains as though they were their full-sized proto-types.

We will be looking into this in more detail in later chapters. There is a more serious objection to the train set pattern oval scheme – it takes up a lot of room. In 00 gauge you need a minimum area of around 2400 x 1200 mm (8ft x 4ft). While this happens to be the size of a standard sheet of man-made board, it is far too large to fit comfortably into any room in a normal British home. Figure 2/1 shows how, in a typical spare room, the baseboard occupies so much room that there is space for little else. The resulting contraption is too heavy to be comfortably carried, even by two strong adults, and much too large to take through a normal door opening into a normal width corridor.

It is much better to use a number of relatively small baseboard units, joined together to form a large assembly. Figure 2/2 shows how a point-to-point layout can be fitted into the same room and leave sufficient space to allow it to be used as a spare bedroom as well. The sectional units

Figure 2/1. **This solid 8ft x 4ft baseboard is typical of many a beginner's idea for a model railway layout in a spare bedroom. The model dominates the room, there is little room for anything else. It occupies less than half the available space in an inefficient manner.**

Figure 2/2. **An L-shaped layout in the same spare room occupies far less space and leaves room for some furniture. The unused space between the door and window will take a single bed. The room can serve, in addition, as a guest room or a teenager's room.**

are particularly important when the model railway has to be fitted into the living space in the home, since it is vital to be able to dismantle the model from time to time so that the room may be redecorated.

It is equally important to be able to store the model safely. As we shall see, these relatively small units can be stacked one above the other. Often the layout is normally stored in this fashion and only erected for running sessions. It is essential that the erection and dismantling can be carried out single handed since the presence of a willing helper cannot be guaranteed.

The largest size for a baseboard unit that can be conveniently taken single handed through a normal sized doorway is about 4ft x 2ft. In practice something smaller will be found more convenient, a length of 3ft 3in or 1 metre will allow the units to be loaded into the back of a small hatchback car, while at the same time such units can usually be found houseroom.

The assembly of a simple baseboard unit is shown in Figure 2/3. It comprises two longitudinal side frames, two end members and a central cross brace with a ply top surface. The materials required can be bought in any DIY store. Framing is made from 35mm x 19mm softwood, normally sold in packs of eight lengths at 2.3 or 2.7 metres long. The tops are cut from 6mm ply, this can be bought in 1200 x 600mm (4ft x 2ft) and 1200 x 1200mm (4ft x 4ft) sizes, though this is normally given in millimetres. These smaller units are easier to carry home on a roof rack than the full 8ft x 4ft sheet. To secure the framing you need 1½in x No 8 countersunk woodscrews, while ¾in x No 4 countersunk screws are needed to fix the tops down. These should be bought in 200 packs rather than the

smaller 25-30 capacity packs. You will also need a bottle of woodworking adhesive.

The carpentry involved is elementary and well within the capacity of any determined individual. Although a separate, well-equipped workshop can speed the process, the job can be carried out with a few common tools, all of which will be needed for household maintenance. You don't even need a workbench or vice, a solid, flat-topped wooden kitchen stool will suffice. The essential tools are a tenon saw, a carpenter's square, a steel measuring tape, a drill and a selection of bits, a screwdriver and a marking instrument. A cheap ballpoint pen will do the job, though a carpenter's pencil is cheap enough and slightly superior.

This is very basic and a few extras will come in useful. A countersunk bit for the drill will make for a neater job. A Stanley knife will be found useful for fine adjustments. A mitre block will ensure accurate square cuts though your timber. A long straightedge will make marking out the top surface a lot less fraught. A couple of G clamps and one corner clamp will be extremely useful for holding bits of wood together prior to screwing them together.

We begin by cutting the 36 x 19mm timber framing to length. The side members should be exactly the same size, cut to the length of the baseboard. Similarly, the cross members must also be equal in length. While this can be calculated, the exact width of the timber may vary slightly from its nominal size. It is best to measure the actual timbers and deduct twice their thickness from the baseboard width to arrive at the length of the cross members. Unless all cross timbers are equal in length and, even more important, the ends are

square, the framing will be warped.

While it is not too difficult to cut this relatively small section timber at a precise right angle, using pencilled marks made with the square as a guide, most will prefer to use a mitre block to guide the saw. Even better is the mitre saw, where not only is the blade kept at the correct angle by guides, but a built-in length gauge allows

Figure 2/3

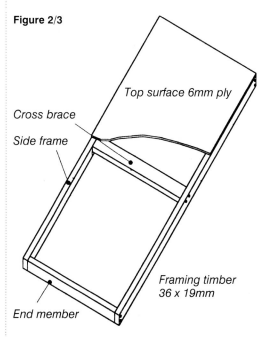

Figure 2/3. **The basic baseboard unit, a simple rectangular frame covered with plywood.**

Figure 2/4. **Location of screws for baseboard frame joints. On the right is a home made marking gauge which will simplify marking out. (see page 10)**

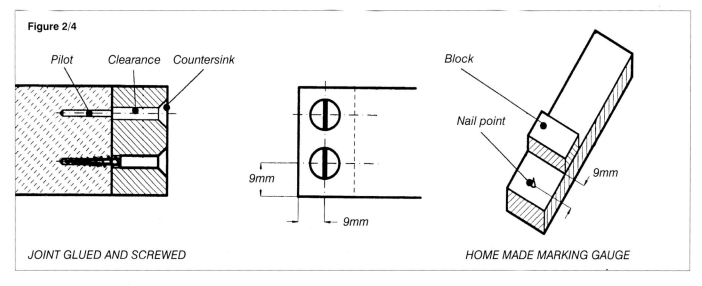

Figure 2/4

Pilot   Clearance   Countersink

Block

Nail point

9mm

9mm

9mm

9mm

JOINT GLUED AND SCREWED

HOME MADE MARKING GAUGE

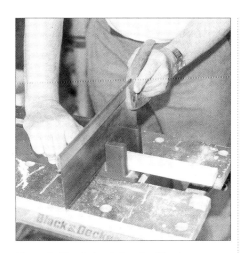

Above: **Cutting timber to length with a tenon saw, using a mitre box to ensure a square cut. The work is being carried out on a 'Workmate' portable workbench, arguably the most useful workshop accessory so far offered to amateurs – so good that professionals use it.**

Above: **The mitre saw is ideally suited to baseboard construction, here it is seen cutting a cross member, using the length gauge to ensure precision. The timber is clamped in place, the saw is positioned in guides. Reasonable in cost, its only drawback is bulk.**

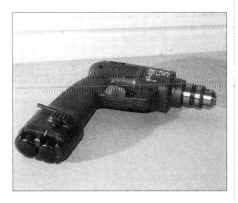

Above: **A power drill reduces the amount of effort needed to produce screw holes. This cordless drill can also be used as a power screwdriver. The convenience of having no trailing lead must be offset against the need periodically to recharge the batteries.**

cross members to be cut to within half a millimetre of a chosen size. Furthermore, it is a simple matter to clamp two pieces of timber together to ensure that they are both the same length. These saws are not at all costly, but they do take up a great deal of room and can only be considered if you have a separate workshop or garage in which to work.

The joints are secured by 1½in x No 8 countersunk woodscrews, reinforced by woodworking adhesive. The screws pass through 6mm (¼in) diameter countersunk (csk) holes in the side members, a pilot hole 3mm (⅛in) diameter being drilled in the cross piece when the timbers are held together. To ensure that the joint is square, it is a help to use a corner clamp. These are usually offered as a picture framing accessory, but are equally useful for holding any corner square whilst the joint is being made. Apply the adhesive generously, wiping any surplus away with a damp rag after the screws have been driven home.

It is helpful to mark out the position of the holes before drilling. Suggested dimensions are shown in figure 2/4. A marking gauge can be used to set out the position of the screws. A simple home made gauge is shown in figure 2/4, consisting of a length of wood with a small nail driven in so that the point just protrudes. A wood block is fixed 9mm (or ⅜in) from the nail point and, when slid along the wood, will make a scratch the required distance away from the edge. It is a good idea to push a bradawl into the timber to ensure that the drill does not wander at the start.

Ply sheets can be cut to size with a tenon saw, the cut being made with the saw held almost level while the ply is firmly supported (Figure 2/5). When dealing with large sheets – and even a 4ft sheet is quite large, it will often be advisable to support the sheet a few inches off the floor and get down on your knees to work.

Although a joint made by screwing into end grain has an inherent weakness, and the frame on its own is capable of twisting, the plywood top surface ensures this cannot happen. The framing prevents the ply from sagging while the ply prevents the frame from twisting. However to ensure this is so, the ply top must be securely screwed to the frame with ¾in x No 4 countersunk woodscrews. As with the frame members, countersunk clearance holes, 3mm dia. (⅛in) need to be drilled in the ply-

wood, 9mm (⅜in) from the edges and at about 150mm (6in) spacing. Once again it is a good idea to drill a small pilot hole in the framing to make screw insertion easy. Do not glue the ply to the framing, this allows the ply to be turned over, or replaced when you rebuild your layout.

This type of frame can be made inside the home. The kitchen is the favoured site since the smooth tiled floor is easiest to clean after the job is done. Where timber has to be cut over a carpet, it is advisable to spread a cloth over the working area beforehand. Suitable cloths (druggets) are sold at all DIY centres, but an old bed sheet is just as good and a lot cheaper. A plastic sheet is not recommended, it is difficult to fold the sawdust inside and equally difficult to shake clean in the garden.

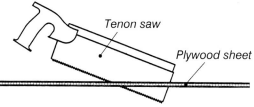

Tenon saw

Plywood sheet

Figure 2/5. **The correct way to cut plywood (and other sheet materials) by hand.**

A wooden, flat topped kitchen stool can be pressed into service as a workbench of sorts. The ideal answer is the ubiquitous Workmate, which combines the functions of a workbench, vice and saw horse. Among its ancillary uses is a support for a modelling worktop. Its value for home maintenance cannot be exaggerated, this alone makes it worth its cost. The Workbox, from the same stable, should be the answer where storage space is limited, since it provides a work surface, vice and tool storage in one unit. It has not been around long enough for a positive endorsement based on experience but it is certainly an improvement over the kitchen stool.

Today, most people opt for a power drill rather than the hand powered geared drill brace and the choice lies between corded and cordless. As the latter type can also serve as a powered screwdriver (and we have a lot of screws to insert) this has a slight advantage. This is counterbalanced by the tendency of the batteries to lose their charge at the wrong moment.

Another useful power tool is the jigsaw.

Its greatest value lies in the ease with which it cuts sheet material. Much advanced baseboard construction today relies on this tool.

As with the Workmate these power tools are extremely useful for home maintenance. While this makes it easier to justify the outlay, the cost still has to be met from the family budget. Creative accountancy has no place in home economics.

Good tools are an investment, they will last a lifetime provided you take care of them. DIY stores now offer a good selection of strong plastic tool boxes at very reasonable prices. It is worth getting a large one for the basic woodworking tools and a smaller one for the modelmaking kit. A second small box can store the soldering iron, whilst another can hold your collection of model paints and paintbrushes. There can be a problem with tools that are needed for more than one category. Screwdrivers, rules and trimming knives are a case in point. The golden rule, 'a place for everything and everything in its place' breaks down badly when there are two logical places for the one item. The only long-term solution is to double up on what are usually inexpensive items.

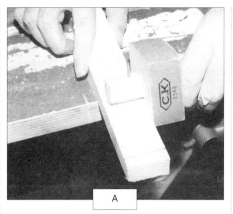

A

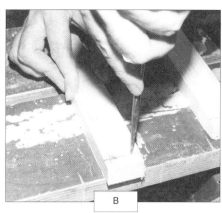

B

C

D

E

G

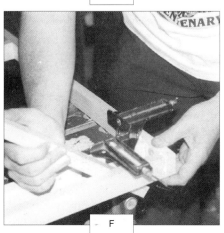

F

A. **Marking out the position of screw holes with a carpenter's marking gauge.**

B. **Pricking the position of the screw holes with a bradawl. This is not absolutely essential, but it does make it easier to locate the drill accurately.**

C. **Offering an end member to the side frames. The Workmate has been supplemented by a moveable storage unit of similar height.**

D. **The timbers are held together with a corner clamp so that the pilot holes can be drilled. A corded drill is employed.**

E. **When the holes are drilled, the woodscrews are inserted. It is important to use a large enough screwdriver, the end of the blade should fit the screw head. A reasonable length allows for better purchase.**

F. **The cross brace to secure the legs is positioned using an offcut of the framing timber.**

G. **The finished frame standing against the Workmate.**

CHAPTER 3

TRACKLAYING

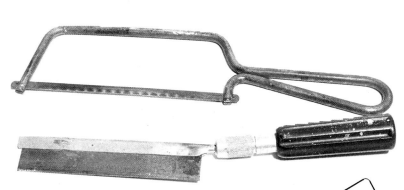

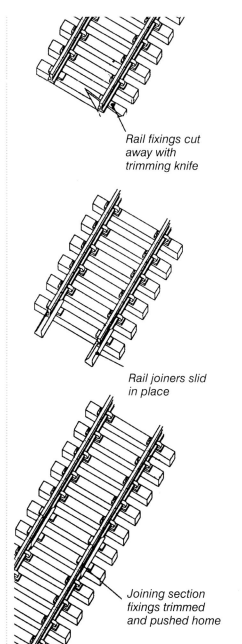

Rail fixings cut away with trimming knife

Rail joiners slid in place

Joining section fixings trimmed and pushed home

Figure 3/2.

Once the baseboards have been made, we can move on to the construction of the layout, the first stage of which is tracklaying. Although it is not essential to do this before moving on to scenic modelling, it is usual for large sections of the layout to be laid, wired up and tested before adding permanent lineside fittings. The reason is obvious, should you need to make modifications, it's best not to have the surface beside the tracks cluttered.

Laying sectional track on a baseboard is little different from laying it on the floor, the job is literally child's play. With flexible track you have to cut the yard lengths to size which is straightforward enough. You need a fine-toothed metal cutting saw, either a modelmaker's razor saw or a miniature hacksaw taking 6in pin-ended blades. In either case the blade should be sharp.

Before you start, you should mark the position of the cut. The most convenient tool for this is a small fine toothed triangular file. It is advisable to support the track when cutting, a simple wooden jig for this purpose is shown in Figure 3/1. This was produced commercially many years ago, but is reasonably easy to make from hardwood in the home workshop. The important feature is the grooves in the top portion, these hold the rail upright whilst they are being sawn. It is very easy to catch the thin web of the rail and, if unsupported, twist it out of the sleepers, breaking the plastic nibs holding the foot in place. There are two other methods of cut-

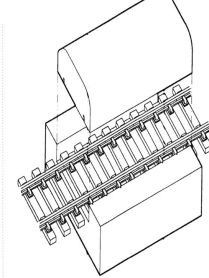

Figure 3/1.

ting track. A thin grinding disc, held on an arbor in a low voltage drill, will cut through rail with ease and since the drill has other uses around the layout, is a sound investment. The discs are extremely brittle and apt to fly anywhere when they break, so protective goggles must be worn.

Alternatively, rail can be cut with a pair of special rail cutters. Unlike the usual side cutters, these are ground flat on one side so that the rail is not crushed and distorted. The scrap length is mangled and, if long enough for further use, needs trimming. These cutters are only available though model shops or a few specialist tool stores.

Having cut the track, we now must look at joining it together again! Sectional track has rail joiners already fitted, and the rail

Top left: **Saws used for cutting track. On the top we have the miniature hacksaw, with a replaceable blade, whilst below this is the razor saw, which fits into a large craft knife handle.**

Figure 3/1: **This simple hardwood device is used to hold the track firmly while being cut. The track fits snugly into the bottom, the rails are held firmly in grooves in the top. The unit is held with one hand while the track is cut cleanly through using a metal cutting saw in the other hand.**

Figure 3/2: **The correct way to join flexible track. First the end fastenings are cut away with a sharp knife. The rail joiners are slid over the end sleeper and the next section, also trimmed, is slid home. The sleeper spacing is maintained.**

fixings are missing on the end sleepers to allow the joiners to slide home. Flexible track has fixings on all sleepers. Some people simply slide back the sleepers to give room for the rail joiners, claiming that it is a simple matter to put a spare sleeper under the joint afterwards. This is not so, it is not only a very fiddly job, you then have to fix a single sleeper in place. The correct procedure is to cut the fixings off the end sleeper.

This is best done with a heavy duty trimming knife. As you will be cutting towards the hand that is holding the rail, you need to take two simple precautions. The first is to make sure the blade is sharp so that you do not have to exert any force to cut through the soft plastic. The old saying, 'you don't cut yourself with a sharp tool' is true, when you shove a blunt blade through anything, you have little control over the tool when it eventually breaks through. The second precaution is making the cut with the back end of the blade so that when it does pass through the fixing, it will be stopped by the next sleeper. This is shown in the first drawing of Figure 3/2.

Rail joiners are made to grip the rail as firmly as possible. They can prove difficult to slide onto the cut rail if any small burrs left by the saw have not been removed. The fine triangular file used to mark the rail for cutting should be used to smooth the rail ends, optionally adding a small chamfer to the foot to ease the entry of the joiner. It is best to slide the tracks together on a flat surface rather than attempt to join them whilst held in mid air.

Before we fix the track down, we need to know the order of fixing. You should never try to bend a turnout. It is made to close limits in precision tools in order to ensure that your trains will pass smoothly across the unit. Furthermore, when you have several turnouts fitting together to produce a track formation, you must align them carefully, taking pains to ensure that any infills of plain track are cut exactly to size. The turnout assembly should be positioned and lightly fixed down first. It is always possible to fudge plain track to fit. That's how they do it on the full sized railway.

Once you are satisfied that the track is correctly aligned, you can set about fixing it to the baseboard. This is where the fun begins, since there is a little more to pinning down 00 gauge track that bashing a few pins in with a hammer.

The pins can be a problem. Ideally, you should use ⅜in panel pins, but these are

not easy to locate on the High Street. Most DIY stores can provide ½in pins, which are a good substitute, with one proviso. We are using 6mm ply as the base and a ½in pin will protrude through. This could be very awkward when working under the baseboard, unless you cut them short with a pair of side cutters.

Sectional track is provided with fixing holes, which simplifies matters until you need to put a pin in a sleeper without a hole. Flexible track is without holes, it is possible to drive the pins through the softer plastic, but it is best to make a hole of sorts. A sharp bradawl will do the trick nicely, but a small twist drill in a low-voltage drill is better. A drill is essential if you want extra holes in the rigid plastic used for sectional track.

The procedure is shown graphically in Figure 3/3. The only comfortable way of holding short panel pins is to use a pair of thin snipe nose (electrician's) pliers. Gently tap the pin down until the head is very slightly proud of the rails. Don't, at this stage, go any further but drive in more pins to hold the entire length of track down. Now check the alignment. You do this by looking along the top of the track, from this angle any dog-legs are immediately apparent. Remove the offending pins,

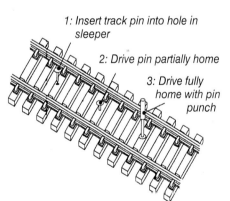

1: Insert track pin into hole in sleeper

2: Drive pin partially home

3: Drive fully home with pin punch

Figure 3/3: **The stages in pinning down track.**

using a pair of side cutters and realign the track. As it is usually next to impossible to look along the track, you make use of a small vanity mirror.

Only when you are satisfied that the track is correctly aligned can the pins be driven home with a pin punch. Most DIY stores stock these, though they may be described as a nail punch.

The usual hammer found in the home is the claw hammer. This is intended for crude carpentry and case making, the claw being there to extract bent nails. It is

not a good implement for fine work and far too heavy for tracklaying. A light cabinet maker's cross pin hammer is a better tool, but the jeweller's hammer is even better. Good tool dealers can supply this type and an increasing number of better model shops also carry them as well. As a general rule, any tool described as jeweller's or watchmaker's is ideal for modelmaking, as these crafts use similar disciplines.

There are alternatives to pinning, using double-sided adhesive tape is one. This is fine with sectional track, but a little tricky with flexible tracks since you don't have any sideways adjustment once the track is down on the baseboard. It seems easy, but is only so in expert hands. It is also possible to glue the track down with PVA carpenters adhesive, but again this is best in expert hands and assumes you will never want to lift and relay the track. Gluing is simplified when you use foam plastic inlay 'ballast', for with this material you cannot pin the track down - unless you're modelling a roller coaster rather than a railway.

Lifting track pinned down track is less fraught than might be imagined, but you need a couple of special tools. The more important is a small pair of side or end cutters. These are used to grip the head of the pin and, if possible, pull it out. Often you nip off the head, which allows the track to be lifted clear. The other tool is a screwdriver or a thin flexible knife blade which can be slid under the track to lift it from the base. This will often lift the pin heads sufficiently to allow the side cutters to get underneath. With care, modern plastic sleepered track can be lifted and relaid several times.

We now need to consider curves. Most ready to run locomotives and coaches will negotiate the No.1 curve (14¾ in radius). Indeed 4-wheeled stock will get round sharper curves than this – after a fashion. However, large locomotives and all bogie coaches and wagons look ridiculous due to excessive overhang. It is better to regard the No.2 curve (17¼in radius) as the true minimum, though even this is tight by full sized standards. Even a 1 metre (3ft 3in) radius curve, generally accepted as the standard for a high class track layout, is still below the minimum acceptable curve for full size use.

A more significant question is how to set out our curves with sufficient accuracy. With sectional track, there is little difficulty, since the units are made with high

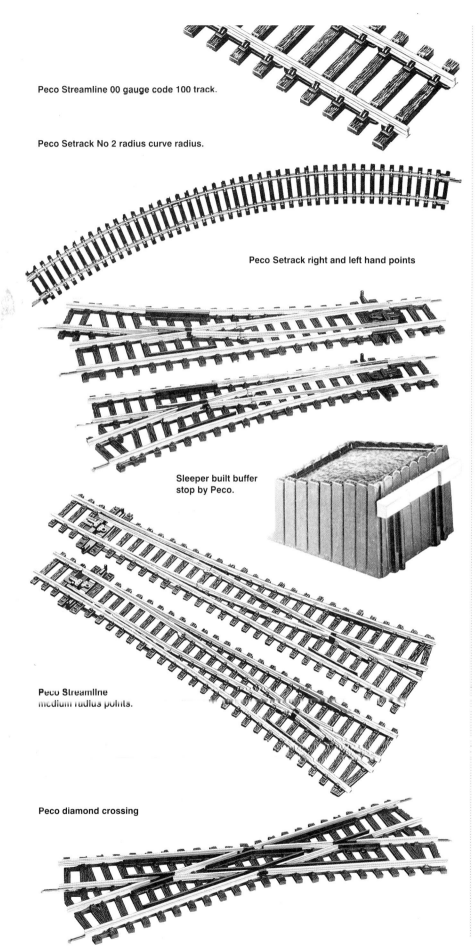

Peco Streamline 00 gauge code 100 track.

Peco Setrack No 2 radius curve radius.

Peco Setrack right and left hand points

Sleeper built buffer stop by Peco.

Peco Streamline medium radius points.

Peco diamond crossing

precision tools. We do however have to ensure that our joints are accurately aligned, for with sectional track there is a little give in the rail joiners and unless both rails are in contact, there is a slight divergence from the true curve. This can come in very useful at times, but it is best to use straight track units for fine tuning track alignment.

Flexible track can, in theory, be curved to any desired radius down to a ridiculously tight corner. However, theory and practice differ radically at anything under 600 mm (2ft) radius curves. The reason is that flat bottom rail has a mind of its own, and unless carefully pre-curved to well below the desired radius, tries to straighten itself out. The obvious method, curving the track by grasping each end and bending it, produces a parabola, not a radial curve. At its sharpest point, the track will be well below the nominal radius. Provided this is not less than a No.1 curve, the trains will stay on the rails, but if you are starting off at even a No. 3 curve (19⅞in radius) the probability is that when curving by hand the sharpest point will be below a No 1 curve and most of your stock will fall off at this point. In practice, if you are forced to use curves of No.2 or No.3 radius, it is much better to lay these with sectional track, which you know to be accurate.

When laying flexible track to anything below 750mm (2ft 6in) radius, it is advisable to slide the rails out of the sleepers at each end and pre-curve them by hand until they stay naturally at something approaching the desired radius. Once this is done, you can then twist the track to a sharp curve by grasping each end. This is best done on an unencumbered flat surface to avoid twisting the track.

Whatever radius curve you are laying, you need some means of ensuring it is reasonably accurate. It is often suggested that you need a long piece of wood with a track gauge at one end and a series of holes at the other, set at varying distances from the gauge. The appropriate hole is then slipped over a pivot pin and the track is guided by the gauge. This is a nice idea, but ignores the fact that the centre of the curve is usually outside the baseboard edge and, in many cases, in the most convenient spot to stand whilst laying the curve.

The correct way to lay curved track to an accurate radius is to use a template, a curved gauge made to the required radius. Such templates are commercially avail-

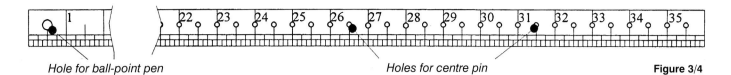

Hole for ball-point pen   Holes for centre pin   **Figure 3/4**

able, the best known pattern being sold under the Tracksetta label. They are not unduly difficult to make in the home workshop.

You need a large compass. This can be made from any convenient strip of wood or metal a little over 1 metre long. At one end you have a hole to take a pencil or ballpoint pen, at the other a series of smaller holes to fit over a pin. As it is necessary to mark the position of these holes with considerable accuracy, the best thing to use is a one metre rule, obtainable from any decent DIY outlet. As the holes are drilled along the centre line, the rule is still useable for its designed purpose, for measurement and as a straight-edge. Figure 3/4 shows how this is arranged. While not absolutely essential, this modified rule is a useful piece of measuring equipment for tracklaying, since it is an accurate straight edge as well as a rule and compass.

As an alternative, a length of string with a loop at one end to take a pencil or ball point pen, is wrapped around a nail until the loop is at the desired distance from the nail. This is cheaper, but a little more difficult to set up with any pretence to accuracy. You can make fine adjustments by winding the string round the nail, the difficulty lies in checking the length with only the regulation two hands.

Whether you use trammel or string, you need to have a piece of scrap material at least 150mm (6in) longer than the largest radius you are using. The pivot pin is driven in at one end, the template blank lightly tacked to the other. The blank should be a piece of approximately 3mm thick ply, hardboard or MDF (medium density fibreboard) a little over 300mm (1ft) wide and at least as long again. The length allows several templates to be set out at once, they need to be at 50mm (2in) spacing. Once sufficient have been cut out, you mark the radius near the centre of each arc with a felt-tipped marker pen so that you know which is which and then proceed carefully to cut along the curve.

You then have the option of marking out 16.5mm gauge with a marking gauge and cutting carefully along the line to produce a curved track gauge. However, most people prefer merely to square up the tem-

plate and use it to set the inside of the track curve as shown in Figure 3/5

It will be obvious that, whatever method you use, the template will not set the nominal radius along the centre line of the track if the initial curve was marked out in the obvious fashion. While one can obviate this by offsetting the plotting hole on the compass by 8.25mm, this is nit picking. Track radii are nominal, small divergences are allowable. Even when the template is placed along the inside of the sleepers, the

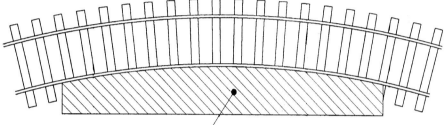

Figure 3/5   Curve template

Figure 3/6

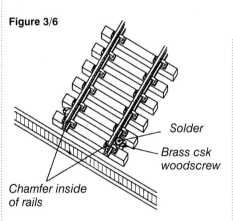

Solder

Brass csk woodscrew

Chamfer inside of rails

Figure 3/4: **Converting a long rule (in this instance a yardstick) to a large compass for setting out track curves.**

Figure 3/5: **Curving flexible track around a pre-cut curved template.**

Figure 3/6: **Fixing track ends at baseboard edges.**

difference, in percentage terms, is negligible, particularly as the true radius will be roughly 20mm larger. The important point is not so much to get a true curve, but to ensure that both ends agree with the proposed track alignment and that nowhere on the curve is there a point where the divergence from the theoretical radius is so great as to cause derailments.

With sectional baseboards, tracks have to cross joins in the baseboard. Try not to have this at too broad an angle, anything more than 15° from a 90° crossing angle can prove troublesome in the course of time. It is also advisable to anchor the rails firmly. In figure 3/6 the rails are soldered to No 2 countersunk brass woodscrews driven into the ply surface. A neater alternative is to use a printed circuit board sleeper, firmly pinned down. Unfortunately, printed circuit board is not easily located

on the High Street and is not that widely available in model shops either. As a final refinement, a slight chamfer on the inside faces of the rails will ease the passage of the wheel flanges. This, it should be noted, is not recommended where very fine wheel profiles are in use. One of the overlooked advantages of 00 gauge is that the wheel standards are tolerant of small errors in alignment.

Before we leave tracklaying, we must consider point operation. There is a natural feeling that it is necessary to follow full size practice and bring all point controls to one place and, preferably work them from a lever frame, as on the prototype. While this can be very satisfying, it does take a good deal of time, effort and above all, financial outlay.

The currently favoured method of remote point control is the electric point motor, mounted above or below the baseboard. A typical arrangement, using the Peco point motor, is shown in Figure 3/7. One great advantage of small sectional baseboards is that sub-baseboard mechanisms are readily accessible, but above baseboard point motors can often be hidden in lineside buildings. The Hornby unit

Point
Tiebar

Hole in track base

Point motor mounted underneath point

Figure 3/7

Figure 3/7: **Electric point motors are usually mounted under the baseboard. Here we have a Peco motor fitted directly under the point.**

Figure 3/8: **Manual point operation by push rod. This is an inexpensive system, using wire coat hanger for the push-rod, and a short piece of ball point pen body for the knob. Only epoxy resin (Araldite) and spring wire need to be purchased.**

Figure 3/8

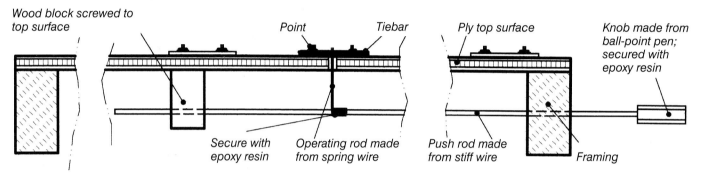

Wood block screwed to top surface

Point
Tiebar

Ply top surface

Knob made from ball-point pen; secured with epoxy resin

Secure with epoxy resin

Operating rod made from spring wire

Push rod made from stiff wire

Framing

Figure 3/9

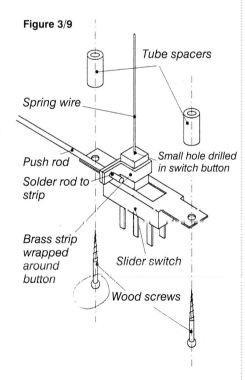

Tube spacers

Spring wire

Push rod

Solder rod to strip

Small hole drilled in switch button

Brass strip wrapped around button

Slider switch

Wood screws

Figure 3/9: **Adapting a slider switch as part of a push rod system. This gives a positive lock and provides two changeover switches which can be used to improve electrical contact and energise indicator lamps on the control panel.**

simulates a prototype motor-driven control, but is somewhat oversize. Full instructions for installing and wiring these motors are provided by the manufacturers.

It is worth remembering that few model railways are as long as a prototype manual lever frame and that in most cases the majority of points are close to the best operating position. There is no reason why the points cannot be set by hand if they are within easy reach, all current commercial points for standard track systems incorporate a simple locking device and do not even need a separate point lever.

The only objection is that this is inelegant. There is a simple, inexpensive method, the push rod. In its basic form (Figure 3/8) it consists of a stiff rod under the baseboard, connected to the tie-bar with a short length of springy wire secured to it, by coiling it round the rod and fixing with epoxy resin. The wire passes through a 6mm (¼in) dia. hole in the baseboard into the point tie-bar. It is very easy to use, you simply pull or push the nearest knob to the point you wish to operate.

A more elegant system is shown in Figure 3/9. Here the spring wire goes into a small hole drilled in the top of the button of a slider switch. A strip of brass is clenched around the button as shown, a small hole

being drilled in the side piece. Both brass strip and spring wire may be secured with epoxy resin.

The push rod is made from a discarded wire coat-hanger, as supplied by all dry cleaners. This wire is usually 2mm in diameter and can be screwed 8BA or 2mm metric thread, so it can be secured with a pair of nuts. This requires screwing tackle and is probably outside the scope of a beginner's workshop, so an alternative arrangement is to solder it in place or fix with plenty of epoxy resin. Do not be tempted to drill a hole in the switch button, this will weaken it so much that fracture is inevitable.

The push wire passes though a hole drilled in the frame member. A simple knob is made from a short length of discarded hexagonal ball point pen casing, again secured with epoxy resin. The slider switch is secured below the point with two long wood screws, held clear of the underside of the baseboard by a pair of tube spacers. The whole assembly will cost around 50p (1997 prices) and not only provides a pair of changeover switches, for advanced electrical control (outside the scope of this book), but is an extremely reliable mechanism that is unlikely to fail within half a century – well over twice the life of the majority of model railways.

CHAPTER 4

BASIC ELECTRIC CONTROL

There is no aspect of railway modelling more susceptible to unnecessary elaboration than the simple business of electrical control. A lot of problems arise because many newcomers ask 'How do I control two trains on one track?' when they really mean 'How can I run two trains at once on my model railway?' The answer to the first question involves some very advanced electronics, the answer to the second is 'Have two independent routes', for example, a simple double track oval. The relative beginner should instead concentrate on moving one locomotive at a time. This not only simplifies the electrical arrangements, it makes the operation much less fraught.

The basis of electrical control is that DC current is fed to the motor in the locomotive by means of the rails and wheels. The speed of the train is governed by the applied voltage, normally controlled by means of a knob. The direction of travel depends upon which of the two rails is positive in relation to the other, this may be achieved through the control knob but increasingly it is done through a separate switch.

There are two common types of control systems shown diagrammatically in Figure 4/1. One combines the transformer, rectifier and controller within a single casing The unit is bulky and takes up a fair amount of room on the baseboard, while the mains lead is never more than two metres long, in practice much too short to reach the nearest socket outlet. This involves the addition of an extension cable with a socket, since extending the lead itself is a job for an experienced electrician. The other system separates the transformer from an electronic controller, which incorporates a rectifier. This is a reversion to the 1938 Hornby Dublo practice and is to be preferred. The bulky transformer can rest on the floor within its cable length of a convenient socket. Low voltage leads are then taken to the controller, frequently a hand-held pattern. Not only is this very convenient, the potentially lethal mains supply is completely separate and only safe low voltage current is connected to the layout. In addition it is usually a simple matter to keep the mains cable clear of the operating area and pathways. Until recently this approach was only possible with units purchased from specialist sources, but Hornby has now introduced this type of supply which means that it should be available from any good High Street outlet. The hand held controller frees the operator from a fixed control position, an enormous advantage. The only good reason for using the older combined unit is that you happen to have one already.

Before we go any further, we should consider the important matter of safety. The 240 volt mains supply is potentially dangerous and very strict regulations are in force concerning mains powered equipment. The British flat pin plug and socket ensure that the capacity of the flexible lead cannot be exceeded, the plug is now fixed in the factory and, in the case of model railway power units, the casing is sealed.

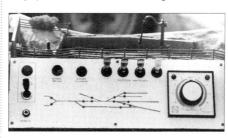

Top: **A simple control panel, incorporating a panel mounted controller. The track diagram incorporates contacts for electric pencil point control, the large section switches are separate.**

Above: **The large geographic control panel for Jim Hewitt's 'Blean-y-Cwm'. The controllers are plug-in hand held pattern, allowing the operators freedom to move along the layout.**

Figure 4/1: **Outline diagrams of standard model railway power supply and control systems.**

Inside this casing the mains voltage is reduced by a transformer to a safe 16 volts and in most cases a protective circuit is incorporated so that when someone short circuits the output terminals, the transformer is not overloaded. Given common sense use, the device is completely safe but by no means idiot proof.

Since the casing is not watertight, the unit must not be used in a damp situation. This is highly unlikely inside the home, but water can be spilt by accident.

The mains leads now have a tough plastic external casing shrouding two or three insulated flexible wires. As cables lie on the floor, they are subject to abrasion and damage. Should the outer cover be damaged, exposing the inner wires, the cable should be immediately replaced, a job for an experienced electrician. Although not positively dangerous in this condition, the first line of defence has been breached. The thin internal insulation will soon be the next to go and then you are in serious trouble.

As the standard 2-metre cable is far too short to reach the wall socket, it is usually thought necessary to lengthen it. This again is a job for an experienced electrician, using a special fitting. It is more convenient to use an extension lead with a 4-way socket, this provides for the soldering iron, additional power supplies for the

Figure 4/1

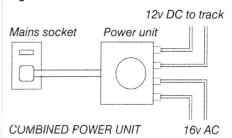

12v DC to track

Mains socket   *Power unit*

COMBINED POWER UNIT   *16v AC*

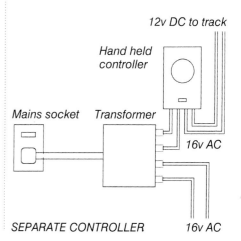

12v DC to track

Hand held controller

Mains socket   *Transformer*

16v AC

SEPARATE CONTROLLER   *16v AC*

layout, layout lighting and even an electric kettle for making tea or coffee. As an added refinement, a residual current device (RCD) can be fitted between the plug and the wall socket. These devices are normally used to protect mains powered garden tools, but their quick acting cut out is just as effective in any situation where mains powered equipment is in use.

Finally, all electrical equipment produces a certain amount of heat. A transformer casing will be warm to the touch when switched on, this is normal but if it should be hot enough to make you take your hand away quickly, there is probably something wrong. Have it checked. If normal air circulation is impeded, as can happen if the transformer is buried under

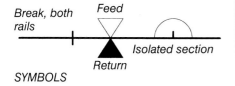

SYMBOLS

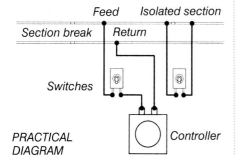

PRACTICAL
DIAGRAM

Figure 4/2

Figure 4/3

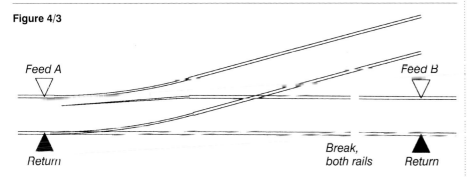

FEEDS AND RETURNS AT A POINT

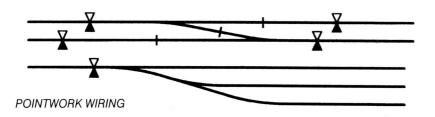

POINTWORK WIRING

boxes or cloths, the heat can build up to the point where anything flammable could ignite.

To sum up, treat the 240 volt mains supply with respect, it gives no quarter. On the other hand the 16 volt AC and 12 volt DC supplies we use around a model railway are safe since the maximum output of the transformers used is not sufficient to create problems and their internal protection ensures that the worst case scenario, a complete short circuit, only amounts to a nuisance.

To get back to our layout, with a train set you attach two wires to the controller outlet, connect them to a special plug and insert this in the side of one of the rails. Any points on a sectional track system will have isolated frogs, and in theory you can plug in anywhere and hope that the current will get to every part of the system. Unfortunately, this doesn't always happen, so extra feeds are needed. This catch-as-catch-can system is fine for a train set, a little trial and error will soon show you where not to insert the plugs if you want to power up the system in a convenient fashion. On a model railway, where the track layout is predetermined

Left: **The arrangement of feeds, section breaks and switches for model railway control in symbol and schematic form.**

Below: **Electric feeds at points.**

and remains undisturbed, a more logical approach can be taken.

Although the 12 volt DC supply has positive and negative output sockets, when you flip the reversing switch they change over. Therefore, we speak of feed and return wires. On all but the most elementary of layouts, we need several feeds, so it is customary to wire an on-off switch in the feed wire. Each section is divided from the next by insulated breaks in both rails. This is normally done with an insulated rail joiner, which is moulded in plastic and has a small nib in the centre to prevent the rails from touching. Never use a baseboard join as an electrical break, sooner or later the rails will touch and locomotives will start moving when you don't want them to.

The various returns are connected together, or to a common lead. It may seem illogical to put an insulated break in the return rail and then connect the wires. There are two reasons why we do this. The first is that the introduction of points confuses the issue and the rules for determining when we can omit the rail break are extremely complicated. Fitting an extra insulated fishplate is much simpler since there is a further complication. Although the cross section of the rail is large enough to keep its electrical resistance low, rail joiners, relying solely on a tight fit for electrical continuity, have a very small resistance. There will be a lot of rail joiners around the layout and if you only feed one rail at one point, there will be places where the line resistance is sufficient to cause an appreciable voltage drop. With multiple return leads, the resistance in the return circuit is kept within allowable limits.

Each individual section can be switched off at the control panel, allowing a train to be held stationary while another train moves in an adjacent section. In addition there are places on the layout where it is necessary to stand a locomotive while another is moving in the same section. The most common cases are locomotive sidings, locomotive depots and the ends of terminal tracks. While we could provide complete feeds, it is more usual to place an insulated gap in one rail only and bridge this with an on-off switch. This type of isolation is provided by a special track unit in sectional tracks.

In Figure 4/2 we have the standard symbols used to show feeds and breaks on a track diagram and their equivalent wiring.

The location of a feed point is critical where pointwork is involved. The golden rule is always to feed current to the toe of the point, or series of points. There are occasions where you apparently cannot avoid feeding current into the back of a point. The two most common cases are where you fit sidings to a continuous oval circuit and at all crossovers, where you have a pair of points placed back to back. In the first instance, with isolated 'dead frog' points, as supplied with sectional track and sold by Peco as 'Electrofrog', no special steps need be taken. Live frog points are not so tolerant.

The crossover is frequently employed to link two parallel running roads, the common double track arrangement. This incidentally is the reason for this formation's name, it allows trains to cross over from one track to another. To return to the model, it is normal practice to provide independent controllers for each track of a double track system, so at the very least it is advisable (but not essential with 'dead frogs') to insert two isolating rail joiners between the two back-to-back points.

Where 'live frog' points are employed, you should never ever under any circumstances at all connect the frog (crossing) to a power unit. This is an absolute rule; insulated rail joiners must be inserted to prevent this. Feeds must always be made to the toe end of the point or series of points. Figure 4/3 shows a typical point wiring in full, and depicts two common track formations with symbols. We will go into more detail in later chapters.

Both live and dead frog points can provide isolating facilities to sidings, in other words, when the point is set against the siding, either both rails have the same polarity or one rail is isolated. Therefore a locomotive on this siding will not move when the controller is advanced. However, with a loop, where you have points at either end of the secondary road, linking it to the main line, this will not necessarily apply. The simplest arrangement here is to break the loop into two sections with insulated rail joiners.

Before we move on to the practical side of electrification, there are a couple of features that need mentioning. A diamond crossing, where one track passes across another without making a connection can create problems where live frogs are involved, but the commercial units you will be using have dead frogs to keep the crossing track supplies completely separate. Commercial turntables provide the necessary electrical arrangements to

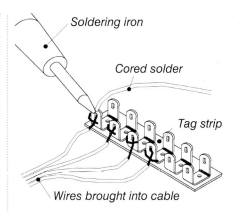

Figure 4/4

Figure 4/5

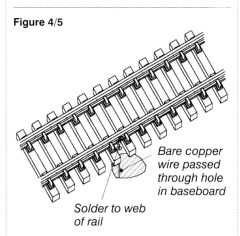

Bare copper wire passed through hole in baseboard

Solder to web of rail

power the table correctly. In practice, neither formation is necessary in the initial stages of the hobby.

Two track formations, the reversing loop and the triangular junction, complicate matters since they effectively link both rails together. There are several ways round this problem, but the simplest solution for a newcomer is not to use them. Their electrical problems pale into insignificance beside their main disadvantage, they need a very large amount of space and are extremely difficult to employ effectively on the small initial layouts that are best suited for a newcomer's needs.

Although many newcomers dream of installing automatic control, this is something that should be regarded as solely for advanced workers who enjoy the challenge of devising complex control systems and find electrical wiring a pleasant way of passing the time. Similarly the electronic command control systems, which replace conventional sectionalising by superimposing a command signal on the traction current which are detected and acted upon by coded modules fitted to every locomotive or power car should be regarded as advanced technology. This is not

because they are at all difficult to install, but because, for the newcomer in particular, they are not cost effective. Although at the elementary train set level they show some advantages, their real value is only noticeable on very large, elaborate layouts.

For the majority of cases, straightforward hard wired control systems are the most cost effective and versatile arrangement. This might seem a contradiction in terms, hard wiring is normally seen as totally inflexible. However, in the special case of a model railway control system, the fact that the track formation is itself fixed means that the places you need to hold a locomotive stationary are also predetermined. Since correct railway practice is to move only one train at a time in any one section, flexibility is unnecessary. Hard wiring, involving only a few switches and a fair amount of insulated wire, is both cheap and effective. It is also, when properly executed, least likely to go wrong because there is very little that can fail.

The essential feature is that all electrical joints must be soldered. The technique is straightforward now that electrically heated soldering bits are the norm. The 15 watt electrician's soldering iron is adequate for our needs, though many model makers opt for the more common 25 watt type which can do a limited amount of metalwork. A soldering iron stand should be regarded as a necessity since without it the extremely hot bit can do a lot of damage when it rolls out of place unnoticed. The holder also ensures that should you absentmindedly leave the iron plugged in and switched on the only damage will be to the replaceable bit and, to a certain extent, to your pocket.

Effective soldering requires that both parts are scrupulously clean. Freshly stripped insulated wire meets this condition, while the solder tags on new switches which are specially coated, will also take solder readily. However, it is advisable to scrape the rails with a sharp instrument – a small screwdriver is the favoured device – since these may have an oxide coating which will prevent the solder from amalgamating with the metal.

The joint is made by holding the wire to the rail or solder tag, applying the hot soldering iron bit and then touching the joint with cored solder. This would appear to require three hands, but the trick is to place the wire in position and hold it in place with the soldering iron, apply the

Figure 4/6

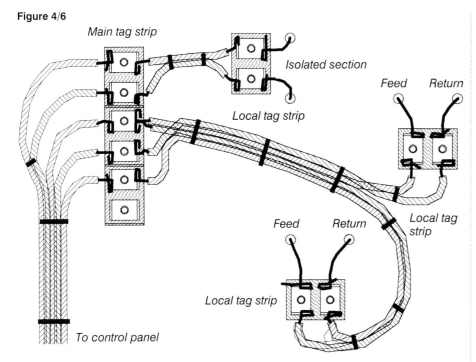

Figure 4/6: **Typical under baseboard wiring using tab strips and cabling ties.**

solder, then hold the wire firmly in place, remove the hot bit and allow the joint to cool. With solder tags it is usually possible to loop the wire around the tag beforehand. Figure 4/4 shows the basic technique.

Since most wiring is carried under the baseboard surface, for convenience as much as appearance, it is necessary to carry the wires through the baseboard top. It is more convenient to do this in two stages. Initially, a short dropper, a length of bare copper wire about two inches long is bent to fit into the web of the rail and passed through a small hole in the baseboard before being soldered in place. (Figure 4/5) This is almost invisible, especially when ballast has been applied. Near complete invisibility can be arranged by marking out the position of the droppers before fixing the track, drilling the hole under the centre line of the rail and then soldering the droppers to the underside of the rails before they are laid in position. This is a trifle fiddly, but if you are aiming at the highest possible realism, (and why not aim high?) the extra work is worthwhile.

You can buy 'layout wire' from many specialist suppliers. You can also buy 'bell wire' from DIY stores and from some high street shops as well. There is no intrinsic difference except that a lot of bell wire is supplied as twin cables, but there are many occasions where you need to run two parallel wires on a model railway cir-

cuit. In practice, you can usually rip twin bell wire apart. Specialist electrical stores can supply low-voltage wire on 100 metre drums in varied colours. While full colour coding is impracticable since there are too many individual circuits, a limited system can be used. For example feeds can be red, returns white and AC lines to point motors and other accessories black.

Low voltage wire is supplied either with a single solid core, or as multi-strand flexible wire. The latter must be used for connecting cables and in any instance where the wire is likely to be repeatedly flexed. Some writers claim that flexible wire should be used throughout, this certainly reduces the risk of breakage and eliminates any need to stock two types of wire. It has the disadvantage that it is more difficult to solder neatly and, in extreme cases, can cause short-circuits when a loose strand moves to touch an adjacent bare terminal.

For neatness, and ease of identification, it is advisable to terminate wiring at tag strips. Not only can you identify each circuit, it is very easy to record the connections to the tag strip in a wiring book. It is advisable to keep accurate records of your wiring arrangements since you are certain to forget exactly how the wiring is arranged by the time you come to adjust or repair the circuits.

It is all too easy for under-baseboard wiring to end as a cat's cradle with wires

going everywhere in complete confusion. This occurs when the first consideration is to use as little wire as possible. This is false economy, for not only will you soon reach the point where it is downright difficult to reach droppers and sub-baseboard mechanisms to wire them to the controls, you will find it next to impossible to trace any faults should they occur. It is better to arrange the wires in cables that snake neatly around the underside of the layout, well clear of any point motors or other sub-baseboard devices. Cabling the wires increases the rigidity of the array and prevents excessive movement, thus reducing the possibility of breakage to as close to zero as it is practicable. It helps to secure cables over 12in long to the baseboard. Figure 4/6 shows the application of this method.

The traditional low-voltage cable is produced by tying the wires together with waxed twine, a technique which bears a strong resemblance to crochet work in that it's quite simple once you've mastered the craft, but very difficult in the early stages. A simpler approach is to use wire twist ties. This makes good use of the inevitable short bits of wire you accumulate, or you can use the sealing wire sold for closing plastic bags for the freezer, or for tying plants in the garden, depending on whether you prefer white or green ties. When the wiring is complete, you may give it a final professional look by using the special plastic ties which give a very neat look to the final job, especially if you shorten the tails when the ties are secure. However, since the wiring is not on view, this is the sort of thing you do for your own satisfaction.

It is at the wiring stage where the virtues of the sectional baseboard are most apparent. Instead of scrabbling about underneath the layout, soldering upwards at some risk to yourself, you simply stand the baseboard on its side and work in comfort. However, sectional baseboards do involve inter-baseboard connections. There is no gain without pain. The answer is to use multi-pin plugs and sockets. There are two patterns which are reasonably easy to track down, the DIN pattern, which come in a wide range of configurations, and the D pattern, associated with computers, available in 9, 15 and 25 pin forms (there are others, but are less easily located). Although produced for electronic circuitry, where low currents are the norm, they have been found to stand up to the relatively high current flows that are found on model railways. The main point to note is that these light duty plugs should not be removed or re-connected when the circuits are live as they will not take kindly to the surges that occur when this is done.

Multi-core cables are available, these are always colour coded so that you can determine which wire is which at opposite ends of the cable. With all interconnecting cables it is essential to keep records of the pin-out configurations employed. It is essential to use flexible cable, the type used by telephone engineers has solid core wires and is generally unsuited for our purposes since the cores are relatively small and are unsuited to our high current supplies except in very specialised situations

For elementary control purposes, the basic single pole on-off switch is all that is needed. There are two types generally available, the original miniature toggle switch and the more recent sub-miniature type. The latter are preferred for model railway work, partly because of their size, partly because they only need a 6mm (¼ in) dia. hole in the panel, well within the capacity of most tool-kits. Unfortunately the switch is one device which is not widely available on the High Street. Specialist electronic suppliers and model shops are the main sources. In practice, most railway modellers obtain such items at the larger exhibitions or by mail order. It is worth mentioning Maplins, who publish a very comprehensive electrical/electronic catalogue which is available from the larger newsagents. This is an instance where mail order can be a boon.

Control panels are most conveniently arranged as geographic panels, with the switches and point motor controls (if fitted) located on a track diagram. This makes it easy for anyone to know which switch is which switch for Ipswich, to quote the old music hall song. The panel wiring is best taken to a tag strip and the panel arranged to hinge upwards for access to the wiring. A long flexible cable to a further tag strip allows for connection to the layout. With larger layouts, the panel is usually a completely separate unit, usually it is only installed at a late stage in the layout's development, Initial test running is arranged through a simple jury rig. Tag strip wiring makes it a straightforward matter to begin with a crude hook up, often involving a series of crocodile clips to complete the circuits.

Ideally, you should keep a record of your electrical connections because you are bound to forget which wire went where in a couple of months. Some of us can do this overnight. While you can trace circuits, using a test meter, this is very tedious. Maintaining a wiring book makes model railway electrification less fraught.

Although the individual circuits are straightforward enough, there are quite a lot of them, even in the small, simple layouts we shall be considering in this book. The sum total can appear daunting if you hook them all together at once. Although experienced electricians are happy to connect several dozen circuits in a session, the newcomer should proceed one at a time and then test each circuit as it is installed. In this way you find out your errors as they occur and can rectify them immediately. Don't be discouraged when you make an error, the most experienced electricians slip up from time to time. Let me put that another way, despite decades of experience, I still make the odd mistake from time to time. For this reason I carry out frequent tests.

A serious problem with electricity is that you can't see it or smell it and if you can feel it, you're getting uncomfortably close to disaster. You can only deduce its presence by observing the action of an indicator. In the past this involved simple test rigs, usually based around a 12 volt lamp and, in the better devices, a battery to provide a power source. Today multimeters are so cheap that their use for circuit testing is almost universal, while all but the cheapest models include an audible continuity test. They are no longer the province of the specialist electronic supplier, you will find them in most model railway shops as well as the major catalogue stores. There are also specialised test meters on the market, but these do not always include a continuity test.

There are two types of meter, the simple analogue pattern, with a needle that indicates the reading on a scale and the more expensive digital type, which give the reading in clear figures. Although the cost of these is falling, they are still something of a luxury. Both types have a small array of sockets, into which flexible leads ending in probes are plugged in accordance with the instructions. So far as we are concerned, you plug the red lead into the one marked (+) and the black into the one marked (–) or 'COM'. The shorter plugs go into the meter, the probes have longer insulated sleeves which are easier to hold. The various functions are set by means of a central rotary switch.

Most of the options offered by a multimeter are only of interest to advanced users, we need only consider two types of reading, voltage and resistance. The voltage readings are used to check if a circuit is live, for our purposes the best setting is 20 volt AC, for although we are normally checking DC, we aren't sure which rail is positive and which negative. With the AC setting it doesn't matter if you get it wrong. There is a 300 volt AC setting which will find out if a mains circuit is live, this is where the long insulated sleeves on the probes are more than just a convenience, they are essential. Although I don't advise anyone to probe into mains circuits, should you feel impelled to do so, the 300V setting on your multimeter will tell you whether any wire is live and dangerous.

The most useful setting is resistance, usually shown as Ohms. There are two or more ranges, but any one will do since we are only concerned to get a zero reading, ie full scale deflection of the needle. In use you place one probe at one end of a circuit and poke around with the other to find if it is connected to the part you expected. You can also check continuity of track circuits. A useful refinement is a common lead terminating in a crocodile clip, such leads are available from specialist electronic suppliers, but you could make one up from a suitable sized plug, a crocodile clip and a length of flex. This allows you to connect one probe to a fixed point, leaving both hands free to probe the rest of the circuit.

I cannot over-emphasize the value of 'hands on' electrification. Once you have grasped the basic principle, hooking the rails to the controller output, directly for returns, through an on-off switch for feeds, the next thing is to get out the soldering iron and start installing the circuits.

Desirable as all advanced electrical and electronic refinements appear at the start, unless you discover that this side of the hobby fascinates you, their snags far outweigh their advantages. Most established railway modellers avoid electrical complications like the plague. If on the other hand you find devising circuits a challenging and absorbing pastime and that soldering wires to terminals and collecting them into neat cables is a wonderful way to relax, then, and only then should you consider anything more than the simple, straightforward system described in this chapter.

CHAPTER 5

'HIGHFIELD YARD'

More beginners come adrift over their layout plan than from any other cause. The main error lies in trying, in a small space, to arrange an elaborate route plan. Not only is this often as near impossible as makes no odds through lack of space, it leads directly to the second serious error, a lack of storage roads on which to hold one's growing collection of locomotives, coaches and wagons. These two factors create the third fault, a layout plan on which it is virtually impossible to operate trains in a realistic fashion, providing a sensible service that offers the illusion that one is watching a full-sized railway. Another newcomer's error is to imagine that it is desirable to start on the ultimate model railway. Worthy though this aim might be as a long term ambition, as with any other project, it is best to begin with something simple yet satisfying. The three plans featured in this book not only provide this, but illustrate different approaches to layout construction.

Our first plan, 'Highfield Yard', dates back to A. R. Walkley's 1925 folding scheme, though I show it in the later form devised by my old friend Alan Wright. It is a very simple shunting yard on a single baseboard, with just two points. Alan's layout was made to fit into the recess beside the fireplace, hence his name 'Ingle Nook Sidings'. As this makes a minimal impact on the family's use of the home, it is a useful first stage model on which one can learn the basics of layout construction.

It is shown in Figure 5/1 as a single unit measuring 4ft x 10in, which is easily taken through a doorway and along a corridor when held vertically. It will not be too heavy to lift singlehanded, a very important consideration, though its length can make it a little awkward to handle.

The baseboard is built by the methods described in chapter two and is about the most straightforward project possible. Figure 5/2 shows how the plywood sheet and framing should be cut. Note the hole in the right hand end back-scene for possible future extension. This will initially be covered with a plywood patch, secured by a couple of small screws.

The back-scene is made from three pieces of plywood. Note from Figure 5/3 how two lengths of stripwood are used to form a strong joint. Pinning plywood edge on is not an easy technique, nor does it

Above left: **'Highfield Yard' is inspired by Alan Wright's 'Ingle Nook Sidings'. The LNER liveried J72 is busy shunting the yard. Note that all the wagons are distinctively different.**

Figure 5/1: **Track plan for 'Highfield Yard'. Hornby track numbers above, Peco Setrack numbers below.**

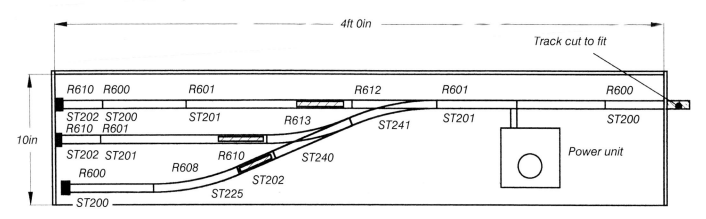

Figure 5/1   ▨ *Uncoupling ramp*

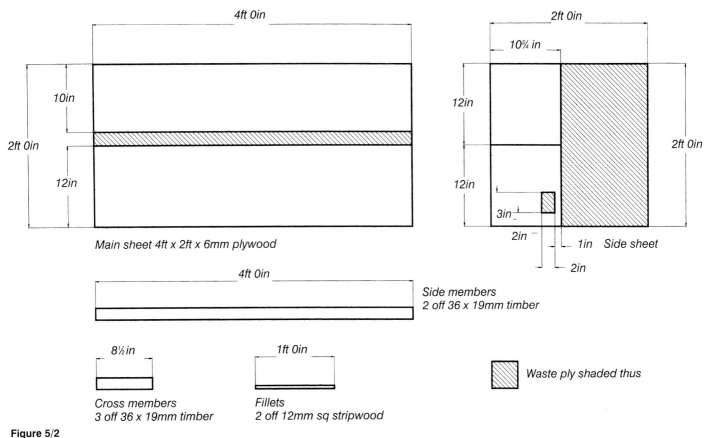

4ft 0in

10in

2ft 0in

12in

Main sheet 4ft x 2ft x 6mm plywood

2ft 0in

10¾ in

12in

12in

3in

2in

1in   Side sheet

2in

2ft 0in

4ft 0in

Side members
2 off 36 x 19mm timber

8½ in

Cross members
3 off 36 x 19mm timber

1ft 0in

Fillets
2 off 12mm sq stripwood

Waste ply shaded thus

Figure 5/2

Figure 5/3

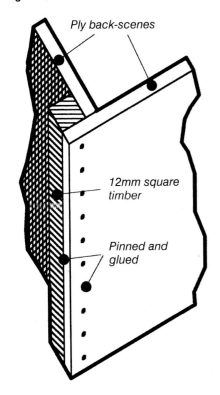

Ply back-scenes

12mm square
timber

Pinned and
glued

Figure 5/2: **Cutting details for 'Highfield Yard' baseboard.**

Figure 5/3: **Back-scene corners at 'Highfield Yard'.**

impart sufficient strength to the joint since the back-scene is as much a protective feature as a scenic accessory. The clearance hole in one end board is covered with a small rectangle of plywood, held in place by four small screws. We'll see why later.

You now have the alternative of applying a commercial back-scene or painting your own. Commercial back-scenes are printed on paper, so the correct adhesive to use is common wallpaper paste. However, the packet instructions only tell you how to make up a bucketful, this is hardly surprising since you need that much to paper a room. We will only need a jam jar full, for which a heaped tablespoon of powder will suffice. To apply the paste you need a large board on which to place the back-scene face down before applying a liberal coating of paste with a clean brush.

Obviously, you trim any unprinted selvedges from the back-scene before pasting. You should also offer up the individual sheets before assembly to ensure you will get a neat join. Once pasted, you should apply the sheet to the ply back-scene and then smooth it down to eliminate any air bubbles. A clean stiff brush is best for this purpose. Wallpaper paste has a good slip and so there is ample time for

fine adjustment. Carry the back-scene around the internal corners to help minimise the effect of the joint. If you feel adventurous, apply a card coving to round out the curve before pasting the back-scene in place. Empty breakfast cereal packets are ideal for this purpose. You don't need a true radial curve, but the nearer you can get to this ideal the better. It is probable that the sheets will overlap the back-scene, but wait 24 hours for the paste to dry before trimming with a sharp knife.

Painting a back-scene is nowhere near as difficult as it first appears. You begin by covering the ply with light blue emulsion paint. Unless you also want to decorate a wall in this colour, you will not need a standard tin, one of those small trial pots will suffice. Indeed, you can stock up with the greens and browns you will use for the landscape at the same time. Emulsion paint is water based and easy to wash out under the tap and is a thick paint. This makes it ideal for priming an absorbent surface, which is what we are doing when we apply a sky tint all over.

You will be better advised to use artist's acrylic paint for any hills and fields. It is easier to mix on an improvised pallet, such as an old saucer or a spare ceramic wall tile. You will find acrylic paints useful for the scenic side of the layout, they are very versatile, dry without a gloss effect and, best of all, use water as a medium. As it is very cheap and readily available, as well as being the least toxic of all paint mediums it has much to recommend it. We will look in more detail at scenic treatments in later chapters, for the moment we'll stop with the back-scene.

The straightforward single unit construction makes this layout a suitable initial effort and accordingly I have shown it laid with sectional track. There is a small problem in that standard units cannot be readily arranged to fit precisely within the 4ft length of the baseboard. The solution is to take a metal cutting saw to the offending piece and reduce it to fit, modern sectional track is quite amenable to this treatment. The location of uncoupling ramps is shown and both the Peco and Hornby part numbers are given. Push rod point control is fine for this simple layout.

Electrification is basic in the extreme. A small combined power unit is fitted on the blank space in front of the shunting spur. The two wires from this are taken directly to the track by a standard connector. That's it. Plug the unit into a wall socket – which you will almost certainly need an extension lead to reach – put the locomotive and wagons onto the track and away you go.

We have not so far thought about support. Hopefully there will be a convenient table, bookcase or low cupboard or chest that can provide support. Alternatively a pair of bolt on legs can be made.

You will need one small six-wheeled shunting locomotive, steam or diesel outline, together with an assortment of wagons. Most British 00 gauge ready to run rolling stock has compatible auto couplings fitted, though for absolutely impeccable operation a single pattern should be standardised. Three uncoupling ramps are fitted, one to each siding.

Most British ready-to-run 00 gauge mod-

els are fitted with the tension lock coupling. This device was first used on A.R.Walkley's 1926 shunting yard on which this plan is based, though in a more basic form using bent wire.

The principle of operation is shown in Figure 5/4. When the wagons are being pulled, the hooks engage with a small inner projection in the loop, so that when in tension, the coupling is locked. The hooks depress the spring ramp as they pass over it. When the wagons are pushed onto the ramp, the hooks are disengaged and lifted by the ramp. If the train is pushed further across the ramp then the hooks drop down and will re-engage when the locomotive is reversed. If the reversal takes place while a pair of hooks are raised by the ramp, the wagons are uncoupled at this point. It is a simple and very effective device which also acts as a buffer when the train is being pushed.

Below: **J72 0-6-0 in LNER livery crossing the road bridge on Alan Wright's 'Ingle Nook Sidings'.**

There are other forms of coupling. A very popular type is an inverted form of the tension lock sold by Model Railway Signal Engineering under the name 'Sprat and Winkle' and is operated by a magnet sunk in the track. In its latest form it provides advance uncoupling, one electro magnet just before the first point disengages the couplings while they are being pushed across. They remain uncoupled for as long as the train is being pushed. The coupling comes as brass etchings and a good deal of work is involved in assembling and fitting.

Another pattern is the Kaydee. This is an American product which simulates the prototype buckeye coupling. It too is magnetically operated and provides advanced uncoupling. It needs care in assembly and fitting, but is very robust and realistic.

A third type, the Alex Jackson, is made from spring wire in the home workshop. Until recently this was difficult but jigs are now available to simplify the process and ensure uniformity. Mainly used by advanced modellers, it is remarkably unobtrusive. So much so that when viewed at eye level the train appears to be travelling along without any visible means of connection. More than any other coupling, it demands precise alignment, but has a strong following since, like the girl in the poem, when it is good it is very very good. The rest of the poem also applies.

The Peco Simplex coupling has fallen from popularity in recent years, largely due to the demise of the Hornby Dublo system which fitted it as standard. It has been transformed by the development of magnetic uncoupling.

While I certainly do not advise a newcomer to change couplings, 'Highfield Yard' is an excellent test bed for a coupling system. Anyone contemplating a change would be well advised to build it and fit the new device to a few wagons and one locomotive before undertaking a massive refit. The reason so many coupling devices are in production is that we are still a long way away from the perfect auto coupling.

Initially, you can have a lot of fun on 'Highfield Yard' just shunting the wagons around the sidings. For more sustained interest you need a little challenge, this is provided by preselecting the order of wagons. To do this you need to have a card or token representing every wagon in your stock. Alan Wright, who devised this approach, used tiddlywinks, marked with an indelible pen. The tokens are placed in

Above: **The Ingle Nook, the model inn on Alan Wright's 'Ingle Nook Sidings'. Well in the running for the title of 'Smallest Inn in 4mm scale', the model shows how attention to detail gives life to the model. Note how the three figures are arranged as a gossiping group and so explain their static nature. The inn's name is produced from a set of commercial plastic letters, the inn sign is however scratch built.**

a box, shaken and then selected, up to the number needed to fill the shunting spur together with the locomotive. The train then has to be made up in exactly the order drawn from the box. This looks easy, but since the wagons will be randomly distributed and you can only get a very limited number on the shunting spur in each shunt, it can be difficult to work out the minimum number of moves to get the wagons into the correct order. The difficulty will be increased when the three sidings are completely full before shunting begins. The operation of 'Highfield Yard' is the exact antithesis of the simple train set oval.

Even with elaborate scenic development, it is a very simple project and before long you will want to move on to something more ambitious. However, 'Highfield Yard' need not be scrapped, since the hole in the end back-scene, which we covered with a plywood patch, can be used to link the model to a more ambitious scheme. There is always use for a separate goods yard.

Figure 5/4 Tension lock couplings

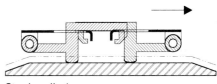

Stock pulled over ramp, ramp depressed

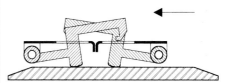

Stock pushed over ramp, couplings raised

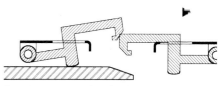

Stock uncoupled, train draws away

Figure 5/4: **The operation of the tension lock coupling.**

Top: **Couplings passing over the depressed ramp are unaffected by it.**

Centre: **With the ramp raised the couplings are separated as they pass over it. If the vehicles are to be uncoupled they are stopped at this point.**

Bottom: **The loco draws the rest of the train away from the part which is to be uncoupled.**

CHAPTER 6

'WESTLEIGH'

Our second layout exploits the virtues of the sectional layout built on small modules. 'Westleigh', follows a well-tried formula, a branch terminus leading to a sector plate fiddle yard.

The track formation is loosely based on the layout at Easton on the Isle of Portland. For our purposes I have turned the layout of the prototype around. In reality the line to Portland and Weymouth ran from the end of the shunting neck, the track beyond the overbridge was extended to serve the stone quarries. In the model, the bridge forms a scenic break and marks the division between the model proper and the fiddle yard, which not merely represents the rest of the branch, it is also the connection to the rest of the railway system.

Although it is tempting to consider making a model of Easton itself, this is not quite as simple as it might appear since passenger services were withdrawn in 1952 and the branch closed completely in 1965. Although there is an excellent book which covers the line, *Branch lines around Weymouth* (Middleton Press, 1989, ISBN 0-906520-65-7), which features the route, the many illustrations of the station do not show the road side of the long demolished station building. To compound the problem, the station's L-shaped structure is distinctive, it would be difficult to modify a readily available kit of station buildings to the prototypes unusual design. As a result you would immediately be involved in tedious original research with no guarantee of success.

The layout in Figure 6/1, below, shows the terminus laid out of three 3ft 3in x 14in

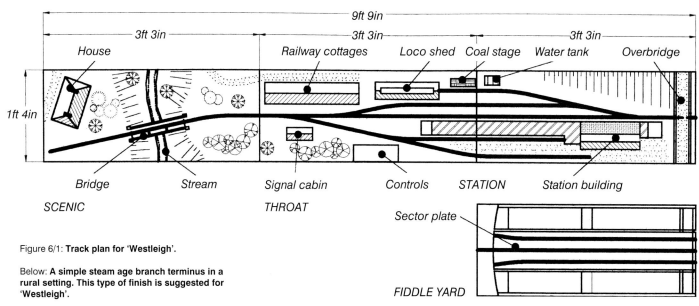

Figure 6/1: **Track plan for 'Westleigh'.**

Below: **A simple steam age branch terminus in a rural setting. This type of finish is suggested for 'Westleigh'.**

Figure 6/2

Figure 6/3

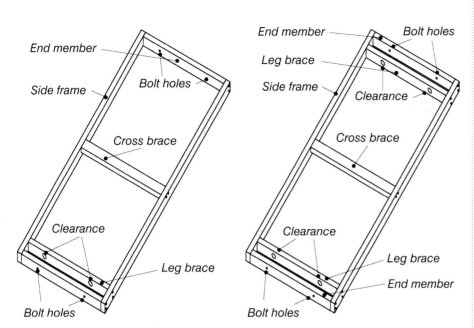

baseboard units which I have called station, throat and scenic for ease of identification. A fourth unit carries the 3ft long three road sector plate that forms the fiddle yard. The units are built on a standardised frame and supported on a standard plug-in leg. With an overall length of 13 feet it could prove troublesome inside the home, but there is ample room to erect it inside a standard 16ft x 8ft garage when the car is standing on the drive. When dismantled, the four units can be stacked along the

rear wall, this will only prove difficult if you have a large car, a normal family saloon or hatchback leaves this much room to spare.

The main running road is laid along the centre of the station and throat baseboards. This allows the layout to be reduced to three units by omitting the scenic section and fitting the fiddle yard unit at the other end. Without the long shunting spur, it will be necessary to use one of the sector plate tracks for this pur-

pose. Sectional baseboards provide the opportunity not merely to introduce a degree of flexibility, they also provide for extension and modification as we shall see in later chapters.

The tracks as drawn are laid with Peco Streamline Code 100 track and Peco medium radius turnouts. Should you wish instead to use Hornby or Setrack points in conjunction with sectional track it will only be necessary to juggle the scenic details and cut a few track sections to length.

We will deal with the scenic section in the next chapter and deal with the more straightforward station, throat and fiddle yard boards. They use a standard frame measuring 3ft 3in x 1ft 2in, made from 36 x 19mm timber. The station and throat sections are covered with 6mm ply, the fiddle yard is partially open.

The framework differs slightly from the simple units shown in the previous two chapters. A leg brace is added to take the plug-in legs. This is cut to the same length as the end members and cross brace and is fitted a nominal 36mm in from the end member. In practice, the spacing is arrived at by using a short length of the 36 x 19mm timber as a gauge since the object is to provide a slot into which the legs are a snug fit. Two frames are made with one leg brace, Figure 6/2. A third had two leg braces, Figure 6/3, this forms the station board and is the first to be erected.

Figure 6/4 gives the sizes of the various parts required for a frame and also shows

Figure 6/4

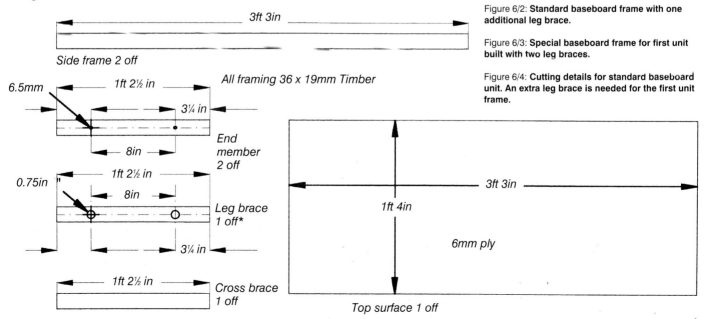

Figure 6/2: **Standard baseboard frame with one additional leg brace.**

Figure 6/3: **Special baseboard frame for first unit built with two leg braces.**

Figure 6/4: **Cutting details for standard baseboard unit. An extra leg brace is needed for the first unit frame.**

35mm

3in

2in

All material
36 x 19mm
timber

3ft

1ft 2½in

Figure 6/5: **Standard leg unit. Two are needed for
the first frame, three more for the others.**

Figure 6/6: **Cutting details for standard leg unit.**

Figure 6/7: **Details of baseboard joint using bolts**

Figure 6/8: **Taking track across a baseboard joint.**

Figure 6/5

Figure 6/6

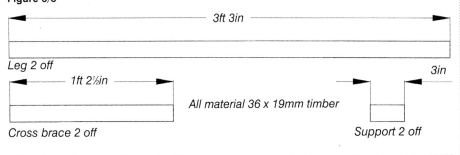

3ft 3in

Leg 2 off

1ft 2½in

3in

All material 36 x 19mm timber

Cross brace 2 off

Support 2 off

Figure 6/7

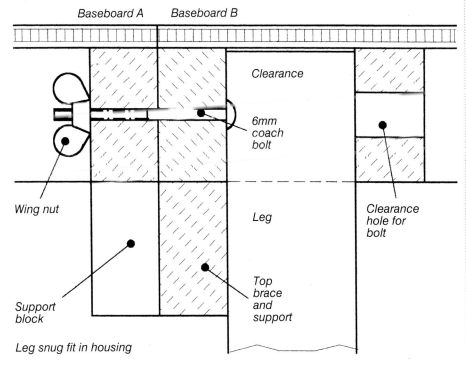

Baseboard A   Baseboard B

Clearance

6mm
coach
bolt

Wing nut

Leg

Clearance
hole for
bolt

Support
block

Top
brace
and
support

Leg snug fit in housing

how the end members and leg braces are
drilled for the fixing bolts. Before we get to
this, we must consider the legs. These are
shown in Figure 6/5, with cutting details in
Figure 6/6.

Construction is straightforward, the
cross braces are glued and screwed to the
legs, using plenty of woodworker's glue
and 1½ in x No.8 countersunk woodscrews. Two 3in long supports are glued
and screwed to the top cross brace. It is
vital that the top of the supports and of the
cross brace are accurately aligned, and
that the top cross brace is absolutely
square, 35mm down from the top of the
leg. This sounds more ominous than it
actually is, but it is essential if the system is
to work satisfactorily.

The station section is built on the frame
with two leg braces and is the first to be
erected. The legs are inserted with the
cross brace outwards, the end members
of the frame then rest on the brace. This is
why it is so important that the top leg brace
is correctly aligned.

Figure 6/8

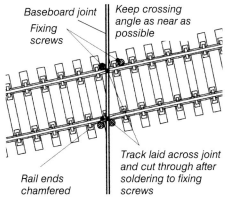

Baseboard joint

Fixing
screws

Keep crossing
angle as near as
possible

Rail ends
chamfered

Track laid across joint
and cut through after
soldering to fixing
screws

The adjacent units only have one leg
brace and one leg. The other end of the
frame rests on the support block on the
adjacent unit's leg. The units are then bolt-
ed together, using 6mm coach bolts and
wing nuts as shown in Figure 6/7. It is as
well to put a washer between the wing nut
and the end member. The coach bolts,
wing nuts and washers can be bought
from the DIY store where you get your timber.

In view of the widely held opinion that
one needs a precision joint between the
baseboards to ensure accurate track
alignment, a full explanation of this crude
but effective arrangement is needed. First
of all, the use of a standard frame resting
on a flat surface provides vertical alignment as well as support. The 6mm coach

bolts are a free fit in the 6.5mm holes, allowing a very small degree of side play. On assembly the wingnuts are only barely tightened at the start. The track alignment is checked, any slight misalignment is quickly rectified by a sharp tap on one baseboard side with your hand. The wing nuts can then be firmly tightened.

Of course, before we can align the tracks we need to lay them. This has been almost completely covered in Chapter 3, but we only mentioned fixing track ends at baseboard joints without explaining how the tracks will then line up, largely because at the time we weren't looking at baseboards in any detail. The most effective way of aligning tracks across a baseboard join is shown in Figure 6/8. Initially, the track is laid across the join and soldered to four No.2 brass countersunk woodscrews inserted into the plywood top. The rails are then carefully cut through along the joint line. Finally, the cut ends are smoothed and a slight chamfer provided on the inside. This will take care of any slight misalignment. One of the advantages of 00 gauge is that wheel standards take into account of the fact that a large percentage of users do not have perfectly aligned track. A little visual effect, more noticeable in close up photographs than in reality, is foregone in order to avoid the far worse visual and operational error of a regular derailment.

It will be clear that the bolt holes need to be accurately located. As we will need to drill a large number of these, it could be worth the trouble of making a simple drilling jig. However, this will then need to be carefully stored in between construction sessions. As these could be over a year apart you could well end up spending more time looking for the jig than it would take to mark out the spacing with reasonable accuracy. On the subject of mislaying items, you will need a small, stout box to hold the various small fittings associated with the layout so that you stand a reasonable chance of finding them again. The bolts, washers and wingnuts are a case in point.

The fiddle yard baseboard does not have a full ply covering. Instead it carries a 3ft long, 8in wide sector plate which mates with a curved end piece (Figure 6/9). The curve is 2ft 11in radius, since the sector plate pivot is 1in from the extreme end. This pivot need be no more than a large round head wood screw passing though a close fitting hole in the 6mm thick base of

Figure 6/9: **Arrangement of the sector plate baseboard unit.**

Figure 6/10: **Track arrangements at the end of the sector plate, showing locking bolt and electrical connection.**

Figure 6/11: **End spacer used to convert two baseboard units into a crate. Two are needed for each pair of units.**

Figure 6/9

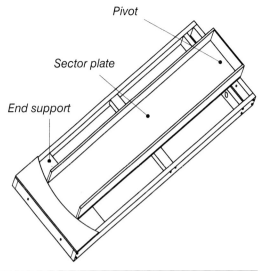

Pivot

Sector plate

End support

Figure 6/10

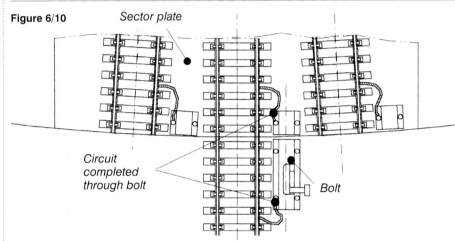

Sector plate

Circuit completed through bolt

Bolt

Figure 6/11

Material; 12mm particle board (or chipboard)
Smooth all edges with sandpaper

1ft 4in

4in · 8in · 4in

6in · 4in · 6in

6in

R1in

R1in

Handhole

1ft 0in

6in

4 by 6.5mm dia holes

0.62in

Figure 6/13

Figure 6/13: **Track diagram of 'Westleigh' showing electrical feeds and breaks.**

Figure 6/12, below left: **Two baseboard units mounted face-to-face to form a crate for storage and transit.**

the sector plate, screwed into a 6in length of 36 x 19mm timber screwed centrally between the end member and the leg brace. At the other end the sector plate slides over a support made from 6mm ply fixed underneath the curved end cover. Clearly, it will pay to smooth the rubbing surfaces with fine sandpaper and then lubricate the faces. You don't need to seek a special lubricating solution, you have the option of a quick squirt from the household furniture polish aerosol or the traditional lubricant for sliding wood, soft wax applied vigorously with the stub end of a candle.

Optionally you can fit sides to the sector plate. An end member is essential since it is the only thing that will stop trains plunging off the end of the sector plate. The three tracks are made from three yard lengths of Code 100 track. Figure 6/10 shows the curved end in detail. A small household bolt ensures alignment. As you will need three housings on the sector plate you will need to buy two bolts, the second has the bolt itself removed from its slide, which is then cut to form extra housings.

Figure 6/12

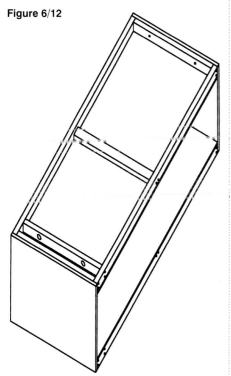

The bolt also provides one electrical connection to the sector plate. The other rails on the plate are bonded together and connected to the entry rail with a length of flexible wire It is best to make this connection at the far end of the sector plate, since there is less movement and hence, less need for slack in the wire. This simple arrangement ensures not only that you can't move anything on the sector plate until the bolt has made the connection and aligned the tracks. In addition it forms a simple switch allowing the aligned track to be isolated.

For storage, and possible transit to an exhibition, the standard baseboard units are mounted face to face using end spacers cut from 12mm particle board or chipboard to the dimension as given in Figure 6/11. You can save yourself a lot of cutting by using a 12in wide length of plastic coated board, but it will cost more than plain board. It is essential to smooth all edges with sandpaper since you will be lifting the paired baseboards with these spacers. Figure 6/12 shows the finished crate. With hand holes in the ends, it is possible for one person to lift the complete unit and carry it around the home.

Feeds and breaks for two rail wiring are given in Figure 6/13. It will be seen that both the platform and the loop have their own feeds. This is not essential but as you will, from time to time, need to hold a train on one or other of these tracks. It is helpful if they can be positively isolated rather than leaving everything to the self isolating feature of the point. The initial advantage is that you do not then need to set the further point in order to admit the train, In addition, the stationary train could move unexpectedly, this would happen if you forgot to throw one or other of the points. This is infuriating enough in the home, at an exhibition you feel you have egg on your face, even if no-one on the public side of the barrier has noticed.

There are two isolated sections. One is in the locomotive depot. Again, the point would isolate the engine, but if the break is just outside the shed door, you can have one locomotive tucked away in the shed

while a second goes to the coal stage to refill its bunker and take on water. However, there would be an additional water crane on the platform so that extra water can be taken on while the train is in the platform. The locomotive shed crane could be situated between the loop track and the locomotive road to serve both lines. Little details like this add to the realism of the scene.

The other isolated section is at the far end of the shunting spur. There will be occasions when it is convenient to hold a train on the spur with a locomotive at the far end whilst bringing a second locomotive off the loop in order to run round its train. This could be a completely separate section, for although in its present form you could not move anything on this section without at the same time moving onto the main throat, when we extend the line in Chapter 8 we will have a section where a train could shunt independently.

Remember that you must not use the baseboard join as a section break, convenient though this might be.

The control panel is mounted on the throat unit, as there is room for it here and it's quite convenient for the wiring. In addition, this is where you are most likely to stand while operating the layout. It can be exposed, or disguised as a warehouse or factory, or a similar structure. The best approach is to fit the panel in first and then decide later if you want it inside a building.

Figure 6/14 gives front and back views of the panel. A geographic display has been chosen, but there is no reason why you should not lay the six switches out in a line and provide a key diagram. The panel itself can be anything convenient to hand. Aluminium sheet can be troublesome since you will have to make doubly sure that no bare wire or connected metal part is touching the panel. Thin plywood or thick plastic sheet are a better choice, while hardboard is very effective. You don't want anything thicker than 3mm or you'll have problems when you come to mount the switches.

The back view shows the wiring. When following this remember that it is a mirror image of the front. There are four different classes of lead, the feed and return, a common wire linking one pole of each switch and the isolating sections. This is a case where colour coding can be useful. As the two isolating sections are not affected by point settings, one wire is taken to the section switch, saving a little wire and a lot of work. Earlier I mentioned that after the layout has been extended the isolating section at the end of the shunting spur can be turned into a separate feed. This is done by moving the wire connecting it to the throat section switch from one tag to the other, turning it into a common wire. This is a rare example of a section break where it is not necessary to split the return rail.

The controller feed is shown as a pair of wires. The actual arrangement will depend on whether you opt for a hand held controller, a panel mounted controller, or are using a combined transformer/controller unit. In all instances you will need a two-wire input, the most convenient method is to use a jack plug and socket. If you are working from a combined unit, this will take your controlled 12 volt DC supply, otherwise it will take 16 volt AC from the floor mounted transformer. A panel mounted controller will be built in alongside the switches and will need a longer panel. A hand held controller can be plugged into a 5-DIN socket.

Connections between the baseboards are made with DIN plugs and sockets or, where no more than three wires are involved, jack plugs. As these are round, they can be held in Terry clips screwed to the underside of the baseboards. There are several varieties of DIN plugs, which will be probably familiar from their use in audio work. Although the Tandy range of High Street electronic stores do carry some of these plugs, recent checks suggest that some stores can be very remiss in providing sockets. Some model dealers carry a limited selection; they do provide plugs and sockets. The best source is Maplins, they have recently opened a few High Street stores but their main strength is mail order, backed up by a very comprehensive catalogue which is widely available and can be found in the electronics section of major newsagents.

Having previously extolled the virtues of your local High Street model shop, it is only fair to mention that there are also a number of reliable mail-order companies. Some firms concentrate on the specialist items, others deal in complementary products such as books and videos, issuing comprehensive and very well illustrated catalogues. They will generally give advice over the telephone and can often offer an expedient service.

In the next chapter we will consider the scenic section and the addition of landscape to odd corners of the station and throat boards. If the more involved woodwork needed for a dropped baseboard does not appeal, the scenic unit could have an all-over ply cover and receive whatever form of treatment you favour.

Figure 6/14: **Control panel for 'Westleigh' showing geographic diagram in front and practical wiring at the rear.**

Figure 6/14

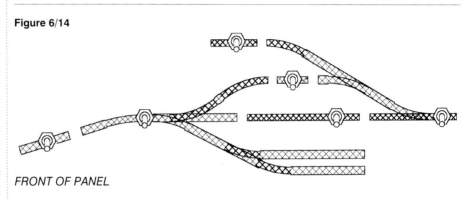

FRONT OF PANEL

REAR OF PANEL SHOWING WIRING

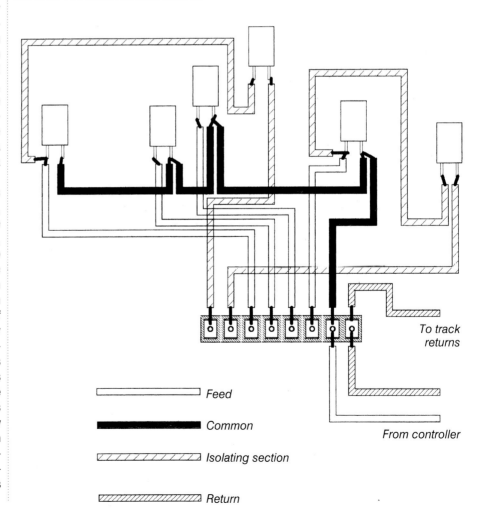

To track returns

From controller

Feed

Common

Isolating section

Return

CHAPTER 7

LANDSCAPING THE MODEL

'Westleigh's shunting spur crosses a small valley by means of a three-arch bridge. This would be unlikely on the prototype unless the line had originally gone further but had been cut back. On the model we intend extending the route (this will be tackled in the next chapter), while at the same time we introduce another concept, the open-top landscaped baseboard. In this chapter we look at the construction of a dropped baseboard and the creation of a landscape.

On a train set the only way one may incorporate an underbridge is to introduce gradients. Although this is not unknown on the prototype (in Holland it is the accepted practice for crossing a waterway), there

isn't enough room on the majority of layouts to allow for a respectable gradient. So, on a model railway we follow prototype practice. Underbridges occur because the ground has fallen away, so we simply lower the baseboard framing. There is plenty of room underneath the model for this.

On reflection, 'simply' is perhaps a trifle ambiguous for although the concept is straightforward, the implementation is not quite so easy as the construction becomes more complex. Anyone who feels the construction is too difficult can opt for a simpler alternative we will look at first.

Figure 7/1 depicts a very simplified dropped centre baseboard, since only a relatively narrow strip has been lowered. What we have done is to screw a 6mm ply sub base, supported by two offcuts of 36 x 19mm timber beneath the framing before we added the ply top. This has a slice cut out along the valley edges before being added. Then we carefully cut through the side frames along the edge of the valley, leaving a gap in the frame which is already supported by the sub frame.

The gap is bridged by – what else – a bridge. As we've only lowered the valley by 42mm, or in scale terms 10ft 6in, the valley is no more than a shallow dip and so our scope for bridge design is limited. Figure 7/2 shows a 3-span structure using commercial girder sides. Peco has suitable types in their range. A 4mm ply bridge deck is needed, supported from the sub base by wood blocks. These will be covered with brick paper or suitable embossed card or plastic sheet. You could make your abutments entirely from embossed plastic sheet, but the wood blocks can be secured with countersunk woodscrews.

The drawing suggests the landscaping, but for the moment we'll pass quickly on to the fascia board. This is an overlay of thin material, ply or hardboard are suitable. Its purpose is to neaten the edge of the baseboard and to hide the underneath of the landscaping. Similar facias will be fitted to all baseboards and ultimately painted. The colour is up to you, for although most railway modellers favour matt black or dark brown, this is only a fashion. It's up to you whether you follow the trend or strike out on your own, though you should avoid garish hues that will distract the viewer.

An alternative material is the simulated wood panel sold as wall decor in DIY outlets. The only serious objection is that you have to buy it in 8ft x 4ft sheets, which is well in excess of our needs. Other than that it is easy to keep clean and looks very luxurious. Don't be tempted to try to get this effect by applying self-adhesive wood finish plastic sheet, not only is it very difficult to lay down flat, it soon begins to lift at the edges and looks tatty in no time at all.

Figure 7/3 shows the construction of a full dropped baseboard frame. The apparently complex arrangement at each end enables the standard plug in leg to be used and makes it possible to bolt the sections together. The framing consists of three parts. There are two very short ply topped frames at each end, linked by a deep shaped 9mm thick plywood frame which is screwed outside the end frames. Ply cross bracing is provided since we will have a good deal of ply to spare after the

Figure 7/1: **The scenic baseboard unit for 'Westleigh' with central dropped section.**

Figure 7/2: **Suggested girder bridge at 'Westleigh' for central dropped section.**

Figure 7/1

Top surface cut away for valley

Side frames cut away

Bridge

6mm ply sub base

Sub frame screwed to main timbers with 3in x No 6 countersunk woodscrews

Figure 7/2

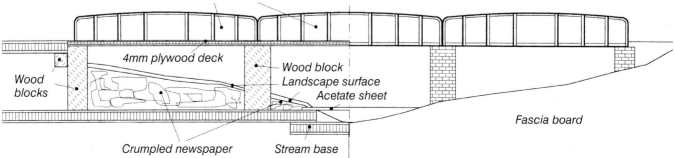

Commercial plastic girder sides

4mm plywood deck

Wood block
Landscape surface
Acetate sheet

Wood blocks

Crumpled newspaper

Stream base

Fascia board

main frames have been cut from a standard 4ft x 2ft panel, This framing will be as strong as a conventional timber structure, but somewhat lighter.

The major difficulty that might be encountered is cutting the ply to shape. If you have a power jigsaw, this is no problem, it will take longer to mark out the ply accurately than it will to cut it to shape. Without power tools, you will have first to cut the necessary rectangles with a tenon saw, then remove the 'valley' with a padsaw. This is not difficult, merely tedious. In either case it will help to have the ply clamped to the working surface so you do not have to bother overmuch about holding it in place. The addition of the ply framing will make this section 18mm (approximately ¾ in) wider than the other boards.

Figure 7/4 shows the three-span bridge which is the main feature of this section. Hornby have a suitable model in their range. The bridge stands on the wide horizontal central ply brace. There is a little more to it than this, since we need to maintain a reasonably accurate level between it and the two end frames. A millimetre or so is not going to make a lot of difference, but anything more will leave a distinct hump or hollow in what ought to be a level shunting spur. As it's easier to put a little packing under the bridge piers than to shorten them by sawing and filing, there's good reason to make the depth at least ¼ in deeper than the bridge.

While it might seem like bodging, we can turn this packing to good account by making it from plywood offcuts considerably wider than the piers. The packing is then secured to the bridge pier by whatever means you fancy. Epoxy resin, widely available as Araldite, is probably the most secure. The packing can now be screwed down to the sub base once the bridge has been finally aligned. While you could stick it directly to the sub base, if you got the levels correct at the outset, you would lose the ability to move the bridge into accurate alignment.

Two ply track bases are then cut to fit between the end frames and the bridge. These are held up by wooden cleats at the frame ends and struts beside the bridge. Alternatively, you could secure a ply end to the bridge with epoxy resin. The track can now be laid. You need to include a short section of track at the end, with an insulated rail joiner in one rail to provide the end isolation.

Figure 7/3

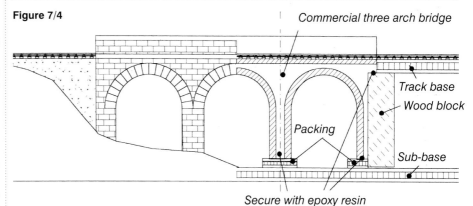

Figure 7/3: **Full dropped baseboard for 'Westleigh' scenic baseboard unit.**

Figure 7/4: **Three arch bridge (or viaduct) for 'Westleigh' dropped baseboard.**

Figure 7/4

Figure 7/3 also shows the profiles provided to support the landscape. These can be cut from plywood offcuts and should more or less conform to the desired shape of the ground. We have now to cover these with landscape. Our first consideration is whether the bridge is to cross a road or a stream, since our landscaping must start here.

The road is straightforward, it can be just painted onto the sub base. A better proposition would be to cut a strip of thick card to the shape of the road and then stick it to the sub base, introducing a little packing to provide an undulating surface, dipping as the road passes under the central arch. This will immediately lift you into the ranks of expert scenic model makers, for it is little touches like this that create the illusion of reality. Incidentally, it will be best to model a secondary road, the sort of lane that has no road markings and is barely

wide enough for two cars to pass. This will not only be more in proportion with the baseboard size, by placing a car and a lorry face to face on the road, you not only create an eye-catching incident, you don't have to excuse the fact that nothing moves on the road. If you like to add the two drivers arguing, you have a cameo which will attract visitor's attention.

There are many ways of creating a stream. We can just paint the sub base a green-blue colour, applying plenty of streaks of white paint. We now turn to the landscape to create the banks and, when that is done, coat the stream with polyeurethane varnish. This is best done in the garage or garden shed because the varnish will take a couple of days to harden. During this time its pungent smell will permeate the house. You may need to apply several coats. Try to create the effect of running water by brush strokes. While it

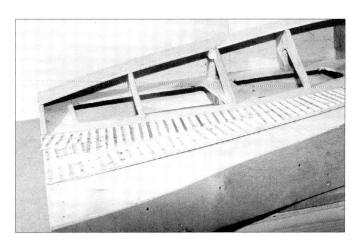

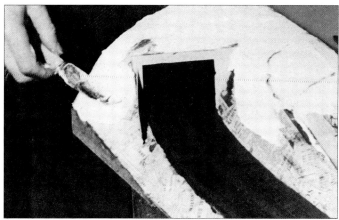

is generally difficult to avoid these when varnishing a door or a piece of furniture, it seems impossible to persuade them to form when you want them.

A more interesting method is shown in Figure 7/5. The stream bed is cut out of the sub base and a further strip of ply fixed underneath. The stream bed is now formed, using plaster. There are specialist scenic suppliers who provide their own mixes, these have improved characteristics which make them very attractive to skilled scenic modellers. The extra cost and, above all, the difficulty of locating the suppliers, makes Polyfilla the favoured material, not through any specific advantage but simply because it is readily available in convenient packets in your DIY store. It does the job admirably.

The stream bed is now painted, using acrylic paint. You can add detail to your heart's content, things do get thrown into streams and once again little features like this catch visitor's eyes. Once the bed is to your satisfaction, you cover the entire stream with a sheet of clear acetate sheet. You can streak the underside with green and blue to suggest flow, but a placid, crystal clear stream is much easier to model and doesn't hide any of your bed detail. The ground surface is now made from plaster and carefully aligned with the stream bed.

We're getting a little ahead of ourselves, for we still have some very large areas to cover with landscape. There are several approaches to this task, depending on individual preferences. First of all we need to provide a support. Except where large areas need to be covered, crumpled newspaper is as good a support as any. It's light, easily worked and you're recycling waste material. Alternatively you can cover the space with strips of thin card. Once again we recycle, empty breakfast cereal boxes are an excellent source of good quality card. These are interwoven in the fashion shown in Figure 7/6.

We now have to cover the surface. Plaster is a popular material, but it is rather messy. If you are going to work over a carpet then you must cover the working area completely before you start work. It is better to do this work in the garage and avoid any arguments. Plaster is normally mixed in the ratio of two parts water to one part plaster, the plaster being added to the water and not the other way round. As plaster sticks to its mixing bowl, flimsy plastic margarine cartons are ideal. You can usually break hardened plaster several times before the plastic finally gives up, by which time another empty carton should be available. Empty cream cartons make excellent measuring bowls. You need two since your powder carton has to be kept dry.

When making a landscape, it is best to apply a stiff mix over the base and, at least 24 hours later, apply a finer finishing coat. The stiff mix can be applied with a small trowel, the finishing coat can be smoothed with a wet brush.

You can instead continue to protect the environment by tearing old newspapers into small pieces and pasting them over the card framing. You use wallpaper paste,

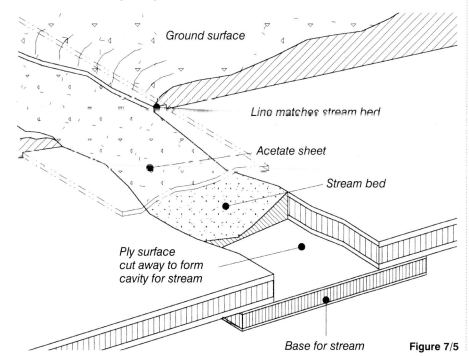

Figure 7/5

Ground surface

Lino matches stream bed

Acetate sheet

Stream bed

Ply surface cut away to form cavity for stream

Base for stream

Top left: **A series of shaped formers which will, in due course, support the side of the cutting. This is a commercial moulding. Note that the ply base has been cut away to reduce weight. A plywood fascia has been screwed to the front.**

Top right: **Applying a plaster coating over a pasted newsprint base.**

Figure 7/5: **Modelling a stream.**

made up in jam-jar lots as described in Chapter 5, a pasting board at least as large as an A4 sheet of paper and a flat brush about ½in wide. You will find a bucket of scalding hot water and an old towel very handy for removing paste from your fingers. Don't worry about the water temperature, by the time you need to wash your hands it will have cooled sufficiently to be comfortable.

You can only apply about three layers of pasted paper before the surface begins to get soggy. It is therefore necessary to let the whole section dry out at least overnight before applying the next layer. During this process you can fine tune the landscape profile, perhaps by creating small knolls by pasting paper over a tightly crumpled piece of paper.

Once the terrain is to your liking and has thoroughly dried you can apply paint. Allow a week at least, more in damp winter weather. Favour earth colours rather than the more obvious grass green. When the paint is dry, cover the surface with slightly diluted PVA adhesive and coat with scenic scatter material. Apply this thickly and press home hard, using newspaper or old A4 sheets of paper. Again, leave to dry and shake off surplus scatter material onto an opened broadsheet newspaper.

This method of landscape construction not only recycles material that every household throws away, it produces a very strong, extremely light and resilient terrain. Moreover, the terrain can be cut away with a sharp Stanley knife and patched should the need arise. The only small disadvantage is that it does take time, since each layer needs to dry out thoroughly. For this reason it is not used by professional model makers, for whom time is money. For amateurs, it only requires a little organisation and a fair amount of patience.

The appearance of the landscape is enhanced by attention to detail. Roads and railways should be properly fenced, this is a characteristic of the British scene.

Right: **An alternative landscape support is chicken wire, obtainable from most garden centres. It is best cut with wire cutters and secured in place with a staple gun. Heavy duty gloves should be worn when handling this material, it bites back and the punctures produced by the cut wires are very painful. It has to be covered with newspaper before the plaster is applied and a second, even third coat of plaster is needed to remove the hexagonal pattern. Moreover, it can only be purchased in fairly large quantities. Its is best employed to cover very large unsupported areas, but it does have the merit of being very easy to form into the required profile.**

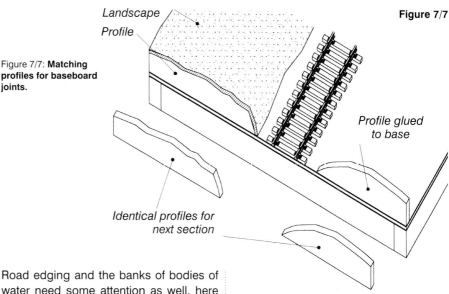

Figure 7/7: **Matching profiles for baseboard joints.**

Figure 7/7

Landscape Profile

Identical profiles for next section

Profile glued to base

Road edging and the banks of bodies of water need some attention as well, here close inspection of the full-size scene is essential.

Trees, shrubs and hedges also form an integral part of the landscape. These may be purchased from model shops, who also sell the necessary scatter material and foliage mixes to allow you to make your own. Hedges can be formed from a variety of materials to be found in the home, foam plastic and sheets of scouring material are particularly suitable. Lichen, sold by good model shops, forms the basis of shrubs, while trees can be produced by gluing lichen and foliage scatter material to a small twig or twisted wire armature.

The fascia board will support the landscape edge along the sides of the baseboard. For the end joining faces you need the small infill shown in Figure 7/7. These infills are cut in pairs from any convenient material, ply offcuts are favoured because by now you should have accumulated a fair quantity of small pieces which are often inaccurately labelled waste. Even at the end of the scenic section you need to cut a pair since, as we shall see in the next chapter, this layout can be extended.

Figure 7/6: **Creating the landscape, using card strips over profiles and pasted paper ground.**

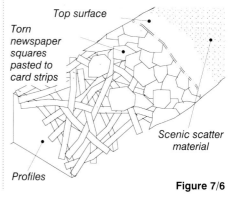

Top surface

Torn newspaper squares pasted to card strips

Scenic scatter material

Profiles

Figure 7/6

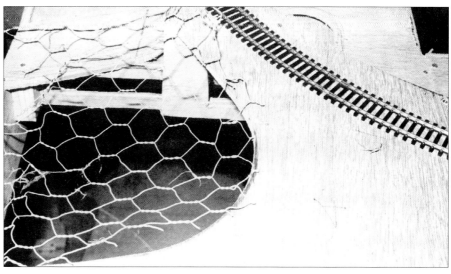

CHAPTER 8

STONED!

That bridge on the shunting spur heading out from 'Westleigh' is improbable. No one would go to the trouble and expense of building such a structure unless the line either went further up country but has been cut back or there was an immediate intention to extend the branch. In our case, extension was in mind from the outset. In Figure 8/1 we introduce some new ideas and, at the same time, see why the shunting spur went off at an angle. By so doing, it is possible to swing a 2ft radius curve on a 2ft wide baseboard. This baseboard introduces two new ideas.

One of the great advantages of sectional baseboards is the facility for extension or piecemeal modification. The modular concept, promoted heavily in the USA is a simplistic use of this principle since, in rigidly ordering inter-baseboard connections so that sections can be connected in an ad-hoc fashion, it adds bureaucratic rigidity to a flexible system.

Although a standard module has its advantages, to adhere obdurately to this idea is neither sensible nor necessary. The choice of 3ft 3in x 1ft 4in was arbitrary, 1 metre x 0.4 metre would do just as well,

while a 4ft x 2ft unit has the advantage that you get your top panels ready cut in your local DIY store. To suggest that any one set of dimensions has advantages over the other is untenable, though individual circumstances often influence one's decision.

With this in mind the corner section is widened at one end to 2ft 0in. This incidentally provides an opportunity to show how the basic frame can be modified. Since this is a corner section, we need a pair of legs and so two leg braces are required. At the widened end the end member is extended to 1ft 11¼in while a short strut 8in long is introduced to join to the side member, which is, of course, identical in size to the normal end member. One side frame is reduced in length. The rear member has bolt holes drilled for the spacer board, since by adhering to the standard length, this odd-sized board can still form a 'crate' with a standard unit. A raking unit can be marked and cut to fit across the corner. This last feature is optional.

Figure 8/1: **The stone yard extension for 'Westleigh'.**

Figure 8/2: **Framing for open top corner baseboard unit.**

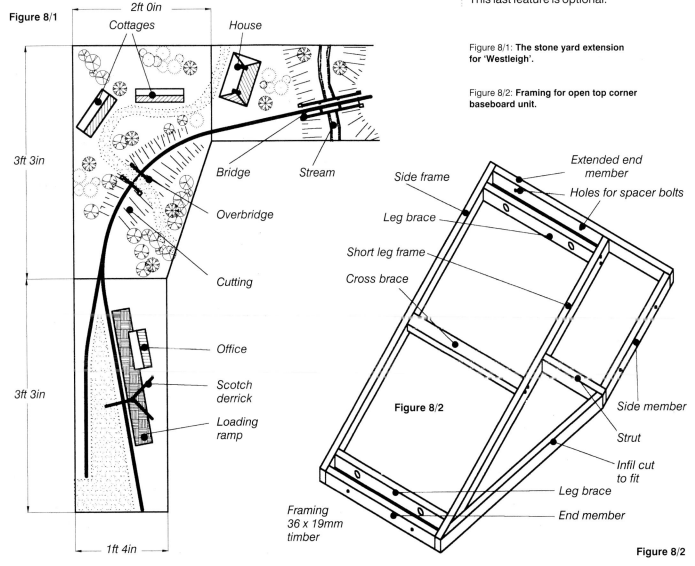

Figure 8/2

The second new idea is open top construction. When most of a section is given over to scenic features rather than track there is no need to provide a complete ply cover. The track is laid on a preformed trackbed, the rest of the space is filled with landscape features. This means that the frame is no longer able to resist skewing strains, but we can overcome this by screwing plywood gussets to the frames at each end.

Open top construction makes it easier to arrange gradients. This is done by inserting packing between the trackbed and the framing, gussets and crosspieces. This is shown in Figure 8/3, which also shows how the road and a 'building site' may be arranged.

The road could be cut from a single piece of thin ply or hardboard, but this will be wasteful and, unless you have a power jigsaw, very tedious. The resulting unit will be very unwieldy.

Above right: An example of multiple level construction, using shaped ply to form the road and river beds. The ply deck and timber piers for the bridge will later receive cosmetic treatment.

Figure 8/4: **Using a trench to turn a joint in the road surface into a scenic feature.**

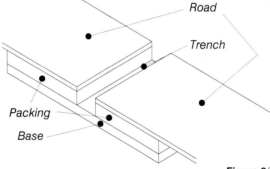

Road

Trench

Packing

Base

Figure 8/4

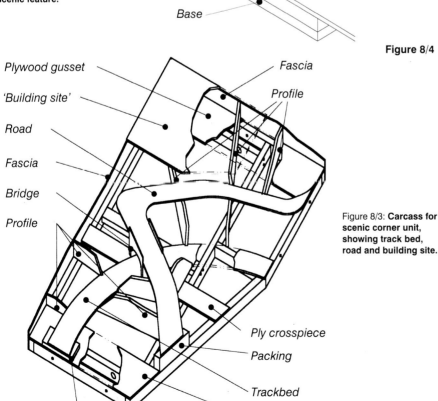

Plywood gusset

'Building site'

Road

Fascia

Bridge

Profile

Fascia

Profile

Ply crosspiece

Packing

Trackbed

Packing   Front fascia not shown   Plywood gusset

Figure 8/3

Figure 8/3: **Carcass for scenic corner unit, showing track bed, road and building site.**

It will be more convenient to make it in two sections which are then joined with a piece of ply or wood pinned under the road. No matter how careful you are, there will be a joint line across the road which appears difficult to disguise.

This is unnecessary. All road surfaces are criss-crossed by trenches cut by the utility companies whose pipes and cables snake around beneath every highway. It's not difficult to simulate such a patch, a strip of sticky tape across the gap will do the job nicely. We can improve on this by widening the gap to about ⅜in or 10mm. The hole could at the same time be deepened to at least the same amount. This is shown in Figure 8/4.

We now have the foundation for an interesting feature, since we can now model that all too common sight, roadworks. This will provide a good reason why all road vehicles are stationary. A modern scene, with light control could have both lights red and a period model would have the men with the boards both showing 'stop'. In each instance, we model the very second where the direction of travel is changing. As a short roadworks should only have one man with a board, it ought to be in the process of turning. On the other hand, a board with 'stop' on both sides could raise a few smiles at an exhibition.

The drawing shows a piece of ply labelled 'building site'. This is where you build the cottages shown on the main plan, or anything else that takes your fancy.

The buildings may all be at the same level, but it would be more interesting to introduce a little packing to vary the land profile. Mounting the group on a separate sub base makes it possible to work on this scenic section away from the model proper. One very distinct advantage is that the group can be turned round to allow you to work on any side, another is that this relatively small project can be carried out in the living room rather than in a separate workshop.

Several profiles will be needed to support both this project and the landscape in general. These are made from ply offcuts. To reduce weight, most of the interior of the profiles can be cut away, again this is most readily done if you have a power jigsaw. Weight reduction on sectional baseboards is always worthwhile.

The final part to mention is the fascia board. This has its top cut to the profile of the landscape. While this irregular curve can be carefully plotted in advance, most modellers find it easier to begin with a straight strip of thin material which is temporarily offered up and held in place while the required profile is marked out.

The fascia is then removed, cut to shape, smoothed with sandpaper and pinned in place, or better still, secured with small screws. With screws the fascia can be readily removed which not only simplifies matters when marking out, it makes a subsequent modification that much easier.

Although I showed a stout timber diagonal, it is a purely cosmetic item. You could instead bend a long length of fascia into a curve. Remember, it is the fascia that supports the edge of the landscape, not the framing.

The second section is built on a standard frame but, since we introduced a slight gradient on the corner section, the track base is lifted on packing. Instead of the ply gussets we are using small metal angle brackets to reinforce the corners, another product to be found in DIY stores. These could be used for this purpose on the corner frame if preferred. Although we now have no top cover to the pocket formed by the end member and leg brace, this is of no importance since the frame is supported by the leg's cross brace. In Figure 8/5 I have shown the track base in three parts, joined over the central cross brace. This will allow you to use up the offcuts of 6mm ply you have been accumulating. Although there will be a gap between the two sidings, this can be filled with a

sheet of material approximately 2mm thick, nearly matching the depth of the sleepers, which on prototype sidings are almost always flush with the ground surface. Once again, a fascia is needed to complete the landscape.

Track is laid across the baseboard join and cut through after the rails have been secured. You will obviously need to remove the buffer stop at the end of what was the shunting spur on the scenic section. It will be more convenient to remove the track up to the section break to ensure you have a good smooth run over the join.

The scenic board will need to be erected while this is being done. Since it has only one leg, the one closest to the corner section there is a small difficulty. You could erect the rest of the layout, which is not only a chore, it means that two more finished sections are standing around unprotected whilst work is being carried out. It is better to clamp a leg to the far end of the scenic section. The simplest way of doing this is shown in Figure 8/6. Take an offcut

Below: **Dave Peachey's 'CGS Quarries', an example of a modern stone quarry in the diesel era.**

of ply at least 1ft 4in long and 2in deep, drill two 6.5mm dia. holes 8in apart in the exact centre. You will need two longer 6mm coach bolts to secure this loosely to the far end before slipping a leg between the frame and this clamp with the cross brace supporting the frame.

Although 'Westleigh' is based on a prototype that was built for stone traffic, I have chosen this industry because it is still closely associated with rail transport. As a result, the model is not set firmly in the Steam Age, and would have survived into the Diesel Era. There are two possibilities. As drawn the model is correct for the early green livery days of diesel traction, with the quarry carrying on as it had done for at least half a century, the only difference being the motive power. The stone would continue to be taken away in low sided open wagons as had been done from the outset. The only significant difference would be that before Nationalisation the stone would almost certainly have been carried in wagons owned by the quarry company. Post nationalisation the same wagons would have been used, but they would have been in public ownership.

In the post Beeching era, it would be more probable to find the quarry completely reorganised for roadstone traffic. The stone would be carried in company owned hopper wagons and in place of the simple loading platform there would be a large loading plant. This would imply a different track layout, with a pair of parallel tracks.

The suggested layout is very basic, with a few cosmetic changes it could serve many different industries. Indeed, the ease with which you could build another frame could allow you to ring the changes from time to time. On the other hand you could find yourself drawn to a specific industry and have the urge to make a more detailed model than the very simple scheme suggested here.

One popular industrial setting is a harbour. There are many advantages, most harbours remain in use as marinas and not only are many old buildings still there, but one of them will probably house a souvenir shop which has a selection of postcards and even perhaps a well illustrated book showing how the place used to look. On the other hand, even a small harbour is very large when modelled in 4mm scale. It is possible slightly to reduce the size of boats by using ⅛in scale. This is made easier because this is widely used by marine

modellers for their larger projects. One reason so few 00 or HO scale model ships exist is that the resulting models are very big.

There are many specialised monographs dealing with rail connected industries which can be found on book-stands at larger model railway exhibitions. They frequently provide sufficient information to allow one to create a convincing model, but almost always you will find yourself drawn towards further research if only to settle some of the smaller details. This is outside the scope of a book dealing with the first steps in the hobby, but it is just one of the many fascinating facets of the hobby.

I have only touched on the expansion potential of the sectional baseboard. I hope I have said enough to show how it may be exploited to prevent a small layout coming to a dead end. It is not just a matter of extension. Existing sections can either be rebuilt or, better still, replaced by different units. This may be done to provide variety, or undertaken because by the time you've finished the 'final' unit your modelling standards have improved to such an extent that your earlier work no longer satisfies you.

Figure 8/5

Figure 8/6

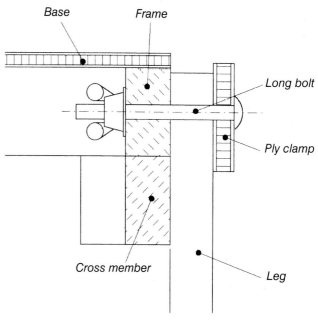

Figure 8/5: **Open top track bases for stone loading yard section.**

Figure 8/6: **Temporary clamp to secure additional leg to standard unit during construction sessions**

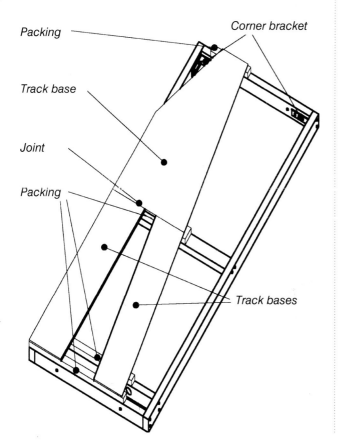

CHAPTER 9

'AVON'

Figure 9/1, is the most challenging of our three designs. Although there is nothing in it which a beginner could not tackle, the use of power tools and a Workmate would keep the work involved down to acceptable levels. Furthermore, unlike 'Highfield Yard', which can be built on a shoestring budget and 'Westleigh', which is constructed in finite, affordable stages, 'Avon' demands a large investment at the outset. There is no way you can break this project down into stages. Apart from the number of turnouts and the length of track involved, the substructure will consume a lot of timber. The price being asked for good quality wood these days makes one wonder if it really does grow on trees!

That is only the start. Although you can test the tracks and wiring with a single works train, operation only becomes interesting when you have at least five complete trains on the layout. There's no great problem about getting them, but some difficulty could arise when you have to pay for them. Fortunately, you don't have to pay for everything at once, but a project of this size should only be undertaken if you can safely budget for a sizeable monthly outlay over a period of at least 18 months.

The model occupies an area 8ft x 4ft 6in. In the modern British home there are two probable sites, a medium sized garden shed or the back end of the garage, the site I have in mind. By taking so much off the end, It might seem that we are ruling out all but the smallest of cars. However, modern car design favours a low bonnet so all we need do is to lift the layout high enough to be able to drive underneath. Only if you have a 4-wheel drive off road vehicle, or an extremely large saloon, would you have problems.

Before we look at the method of construction, we must discuss the design. It is based on John Allen's original 'Gorre and Daphetid' layout, first described in the late 1940s. This was a good compact continuous layout that provided a reasonable length of run by looping the track over itself - the looped eight formation. This provides for interesting scenic effects in a relatively small area. I have in mind modern diesel power, the branch is only workable with railcars while the use of single track again suggests modern secondary line practice. While there is not sufficient room for a full HST rake, let alone a model of a Eurostar train, don't let small details prevent you owning a cut-down version. Although it is a good idea to follow prototype practice, it is best done at a respectful distance. Or, to put it another way, modeller's license is a wonderful thing.

All the curves are No.2 radius and the pointwork is laid out for Hornby or Peco Setrack small radius turnouts. Provided you are prepared to cut a few filler pieces, you can use sectional track throughout,

Figure 9/1: **Layout plan for 'Avon', housed at the end of a garage.**

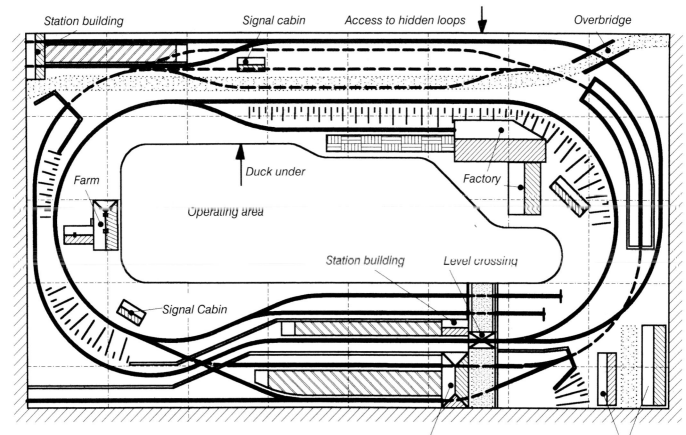

Station building   Signal cabin   Access to hidden loops   Overbridge

Duck under

Farm   Operating area   Factory

Signal Cabin   Station building   Level crossing

Houses

Figure 9/1   Station building

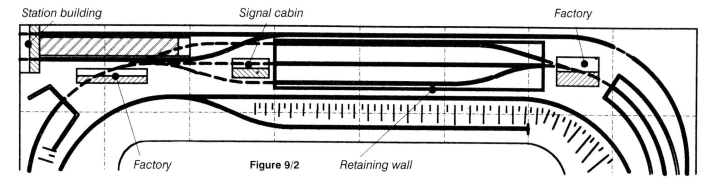

Station building   Signal cabin   Factory

Factory   **Figure 9/2**   Retaining wall

but it will be more convenient and cheaper to use flexible track for the straights. You don't have to bend it just because it will let you do so.

The layout includes a fair amount of storage space for trains. The little branch terminus can hold two twin unit railcars and there is a long siding off the outer platform loop to hold these as well, so you can have three sets. In addition to the three hidden loops there are two holding sidings near the main station and a long siding serving a factory. You can comfortably handle five main line trains, though a sixth would make operation extremely difficult.

The plan shows a pair of interesting scenic dodges. The branch station has an overtrack station building, implying that the line runs out through the wall. In a garden shed it could lead out to a reverse loop for use in fine weather. It would be possible to model the road bridge as well, but this will reduce the visible length of the platforms. Another overtrack station building serves the low level main line station, with an adjacent high level single platform halt.

Both stations serve the thriving town of 'Avon'. This will have to be represented on the back-scene, though if you feel able to move the layout an inch or so clear of the wall you could have room for low relief models. This is something you must decide at the early stages of construction, when it will be easier to move the substructure.

As, in a garage location, both sides of the branch line section are accessible, it will be easy enough to reach underneath to clean the low level loops and remove any derailed stock. I would suggest that the branch station could well be made removable, and that the landscape covering the hidden loops is similarly built so it can easily be lifted off. Alternatively, you could omit the cover altogether as shown in Figure 9/2, introducing retaining walls and girder bridges around the low level loops. This multiple level arrangement is common enough in urban areas to allow you to create a realistic scene.

It would be possible to construct the layout on four rectangular baseboard units.

Figure 9/2: **An alternative version of the plan bringing the storage loops out into the open.**

Figure 9/3: **Details of L girder construction.**

Figure 9/4: **Supporting L girders from the wall of the garage.**

Although two of them would be longer than 4ft this is of less importance for a garage layout, since you have a wide door and, with the car out of the way, there is ample room for two people to lift the larger sections out and into a waiting van, or onto the roof rack when it is wanted for an exhibition.

A garage location does make a permanent layout a possibility, so we will look at another form of construction, using L girders and full open top construction. An L girder, as the name implies, is a wooden girder of inverted L section made from two pieces of timber which, in this instance, are cut to a small fraction of an inch less than the width of the garage. The vertical timber is 72x19mm section, the top is 36x19mm. Figure 9/3 shows the constructional details.

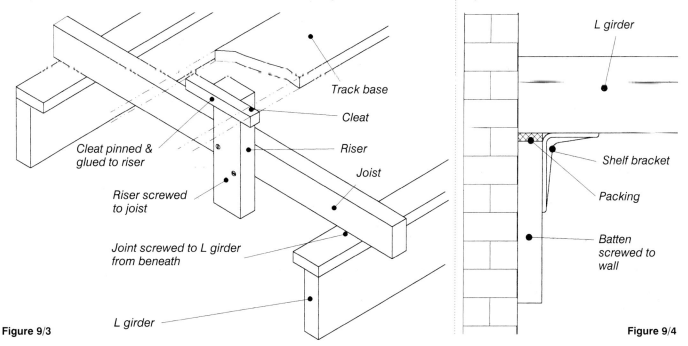

Track base

Cleat

Cleat pinned & glued to riser

Riser

Riser screwed to joist

Joist

Joint screwed to L girder from beneath

L girder

L girder

Shelf bracket

Packing

Batten screwed to wall

Figure 9/3   **Figure 9/4**

The two L girder timbers are liberally coated with woodworking glue and clamped together. 1½in oval nails are driven in, skew fashion, to hold the wood together whilst setting. Any surplus glue is then wiped away with a damp cloth. This is where the Workmate comes into its own, since you can hold three feet of timber at a time for nailing.

The size given is strong enough to span an 8ft gap without sagging under load. Since we have four of them, a very considerable weight can be supported. It might appear to be overkill, but the fact is that you will, from time to time, lean on the framing, or use the L girder to pull yourself up after a prolonged session underneath. Under baseboard working is a feature of L girder construction, but the clearance beneath the layout, at least 3ft 6in, makes this less of a chore than with the normal baseboard height, which gives a foot less clearance,

There are two ways of supporting the L girders. The simplest is to secure four short vertical battens to each wall, rest the L girders on the battens and secure with small shelf brackets (Figure 9/4). As all eight battens have to have their tops on exactly the same plane, there could be problems, so I show packing between the batten and the girder to provide adjustment. Although the levelling can be done with a small spirit level, the long builder's level is much easier to use.

Alternatively, each girder can be supported on a pair of stout legs. I suggest 46mm square timber, with a halved joint at the top, the simplest of all housings. The general principle is shown in Figure 9/5. No bracing is required since once in place, the legs are prevented from moving by the garage walls. It is advisable to check whether the garage floor is level, or if the builders have given it a slight fall from back to front to improve drainage. Although, as we shall see, there is no need to get the substructure absolutely level with L girders, casually to introduce a slope is sloppy workmanship.

A series of joists are run across the L girder. I suggest 36 x 19mm section, though this is not critical, almost any section around this size can be pressed into service. You don't necessarily need to have all alike since there is no need to lay any track bases directly onto the joists.

They are secured from underneath by 1in x No.8 wood screws and are best set at approximately 12in spacing, this again is not at all critical. Figure 9/6 shows how the joists are laid out. Note that the overhang varies to accommodate parts of the layout. The principle is that, when in doubt, add at least three inches. Any surplus can always be cut away later, or you can always move or even replace a joist from underneath.

The tracks are carried on sub-bases, cut from 9mm ply or MDF. Figure 9/7 shows the full quota of bases in position. As all the curves are the same radius, it will save a lot of time if you first make a hardboard template for the curve base. A second straight template, 2in wide, will make marking out a straightforward proposition. Unless you have a power jigsaw, cutting the bases to size is going to be extremely tedious.

Sub bases are supported by risers which have a cleat across the top. These are shown in Figure 9/3. The cleats are pinned and glued to the riser, this is one part of an L girder system that need never be dismantled. The sizes of the risers and cleats are again not at all critical, nor need they be similar, any suitable scrap wood and offcuts can be pressed into service. Cleats are best made longer and then cut to size after the track base is finally in place. Similarly, the risers need to be on the long side, any excess below the joist can be left dangling there as they are not visible. Indeed this might be useful should you need to raise the track at some later date.

The track bases may be secured from underneath, this allows all adjustments to be carried out from beneath the layout. However, you may find it more convenient to screw the track bases down in the conventional manner. In this case it will be a good idea to keep a plan showing where the cleats and risers are located, since the screwheads will be hidden under the ballast or other scenic treatment.

For convenience you need at least four clamps to hold the risers in place while adjusting the gradients. Once you are satisfied that you have arranged sufficient clearance and set all tracks at their optimum level you can screw the risers to the joists. As you have to screw in sideways, it will be best to use cross-headed screws and it is even more convenient to have an angled screwdriver. This is a tool that appears to be a gimmick, but does perform as claimed. You won't use it often, but when you do need to deploy it, it is absolutely invaluable. The alternative, a short screwdriver, is nowhere near as effective.

Most people have difficulty visualising a multi-level layout from a flat plan. Where a lot of curves are involved, even a perspective or isometric sketch is almost as confusing, since no matter which view you chose, some crucial parts are hidden. The classic solution is to begin by making a small scale model of the model from stripwood and card. These are usually made to 1:12 or 1:10 scale, but I would suggest 1:8 (1½in to the foot) would be even better.

Figure 9/5

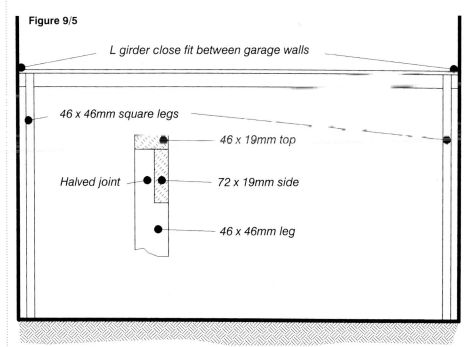

L girder close fit between garage walls

46 x 46mm square legs

46 x 19mm top

Halved joint

72 x 19mm side

46 x 46mm leg

Figure 9/5: **Free standing L girder support.**

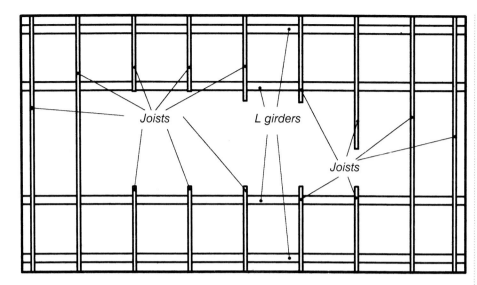

Figure 9/6: **Plan of L girders and joists for 'Avon'.**

Figure 9/7: **Plan of track bases for 'Avon'.**

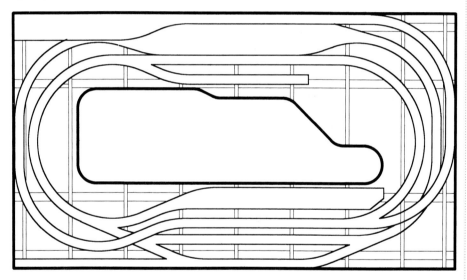

The model needs to be on a strong base, a piece of 12mm chipboard is recommended, since it will be used as a 3D blueprint during construction. Not only does this help with the substructure, the landscape can be filled in, using modelling clay and buildings, cut roughly from wood, put in place to gauge the overall effect. This model can save a lot of time, it's much easier solving any difficulties on a smaller scale.

When the framework is in place, it's a good idea to cut out templates for the track bed from thick card. This will make good use of empty packing cartons before they finish up on the dump. 2in wide parcel tape will be needed as there will be plenty of joins. Any errors can be corrected at this stage while at the same time you can check the location of joists and risers and make any adjustments that seem advisable. Wherever possible joins in the sub bases should be made over risers to prevent possible sagging at this weak point. Such risers will need a cleat on each side to provide wider support.

When you are satisfied, the card templates can then be used to set out the sub-bases on the ply or MDF sheet. This will make it easier to devise the most economical way of cutting the sheet. A power jigsaw will be useful at this stage, some might think it essential but a padsaw and determination makes a fair substitute.

The relatively narrow sub base will bow alarmingly if you try to pin the track down in situ. The use of a dolly, a heavy mass of metal held under the sub-base to absorb the hammer blow, requires a third hand. We need to look for an alternative.

The luxury solution is to lay a track base on the sub base. This can be 9 or 12mm thick semi-hard insulation board, but I have yet to find a DIY store with stocks, and even builder's suppliers can look blankly at you when you ask. Some model shops do stock 4ft x 2ft sheets of 9mm Sundeala. This board is widely used for pin boards, so the track can be pinned down with ½in office pins, which are pushed into the material with flat-nosed pliers.

You can also use pre-formed foam plastic ballast inlay. Generally, I don't advise this since, apart from anything else, you have first to secure the track into the ballast with a thin string of PVA glue, then stick the foam ballast to the sub base which has been liberally coated with glue. When you also have to curve the track to suit the layout design, you have a problem. However, as we are using sectional track for the curves with the rest of the track as near straight as makes no odds, there should be few alignment problems. It still leaves you with the somewhat unrealistic appearance of foam ballast, which is compounded by its unpredictable reaction to track paint.

The best solution is to apply a little lateral thinking. Begin by partially assembling all the sub-bases by only putting two screws in each, one at each end. Then methodically remove each base, lay it flat on the invaluable Workmate and pin the track down, leaving the extreme ends free and slightly oversize. At the same time, you can add the wiring, we will look at this later. The sub bases are then reassembled, the ends being aligned and pinned down in situ. This is another reason why it is a good idea to have the joins over the risers, these support the base whilst pinning down. What you have done is to turn the entire layout into a custom built sectional track system, using large, individual units comprising sub-base, track *and wiring*.

You could even install signals and other trackside feature and erect the platforms on the workbench. As mentioned earlier, the branch terminus can be built as a unit, complete with the station buildings and signal cabin. Apart from providing access to the loop pointwork, it is going to be much easier to complete the station on the workbench than it would be in the far corner of the layout.

Figure 9/8 shows the arrangement of feeds and breaks for two rail wiring. Both main platform roads have separate feeds so that trains can be readily isolated.

For the hidden loops I have shown the alternative arrangement, where the isolation is provided solely by the points. You can use either approach. In addition the terminus roads and holding sidings have permanent isolation. The railcar siding off the outer main station loop has its isolating section halfway down, to enable you to store two two-unit sets in this road. Branch railcars are limited to two cars by the length of the terminus roads.

Since the layout is permanently erected, you can't stand it on its side to complete the wiring, which is why it is a good idea to wire each sub base before installing it. You can then attach long leads to each dropper and take these to a tag strip screwed to an L girder or a joist. There's just one small difficulty, you will almost inevitably leave the leads dangling for days, if not weeks while you continue tracklaying, by which time you'll have forgotten which wire is which.

A better approach is to convert these loose wires into an umbilical cable terminating in a tag strip, which can be screwed in place immediately. This is shown diagrammatically in Figure 9/9. In practice, the wires from the droppers to the sub base tag strip should be neatly cabled and not left as a drunken spider's web. As this cable will have to pass beside at least one riser, it needs to have a reasonable amount of slack.

The connections to the tag strip must be recorded, preferably in a wiring book. A common practice is to make the record at the workbench on an A4 pad. The sheet is then given an easily memorised identification, 'branch terminus' is to be preferred to C10, since a code only looks professional. It needs a further decoding book. The A4 sheet is then slipped into a plastic pocket which in turn is secured in a ring back binder. Ideally, the rough sheet is then transcribed in a neat manner at a later date into a master wiring book. You could use a Filofax type folder, but it's dearer than the A4 binder which has the added advantage of being less easy to mislay.

You could use multi-core cable for the umbilical, but as you will usually find that you either have five wires over or one too few, you can instead cut sufficient equal lengths of wire, join each to the two tag strips in turn and then turn the bunch into a cable. Ties are adequate, you can wrap the bunch with self adhesive tape, or there is a very versatile spiral plastic sheath made for the job.

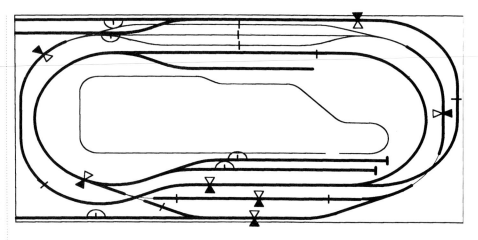

Figure 9/8: **Track diagram of 'Avon' showing feeds and breaks.**

Figure 9/9: **Umbilical cable wiring for L girder layout.**

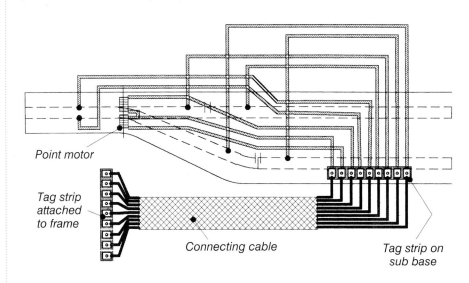

Point motor

Tag strip attached to frame

Connecting cable

Tag strip on sub base

Figure 9/10: **Cable trough for L girder layout.**

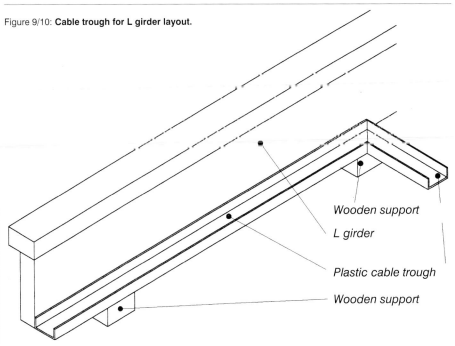

Wooden support

L girder

Plastic cable trough

Wooden support

Whatever you do, don't leave the lot loose. As the umbilical cable will not be flexed, it is not essential to use flexible wire, but unless you have a very large stock of solid core wire, you might as well play safe. It will usually be possible to secure the cable to the framing. You can use long plastic ties, but string will do just as well.

The diagram shows the wiring for the branch terminus which I suggested should be removable. You have two options. One is to have a long umbilical cable so that the station can be lifted well clear. A better option is to fit a multipin socket in place of the sub-base tag strip and have a corresponding plug on the cable. As you only have nine wires, a 9-pin D pattern plug and socket is ideally suited for the job.

This will be fine until you decide to install colour lights. The prudent arrangement is to use a 15-pin D plug and socket, but it's little if any more trouble to provide another umbilical for the signals alone, and for station lights if, at some later stage, you want to fit these as well.

Right: **Kit built Parcels DMU running on the Whitchurch (Cardiff) Model Engineering Society's 00 gauge layout.** Photograph by Tony Wright, courtesy of *Model Railways*

Below: **Modified Hornby Pacers on Keir Hardy's 'Holmeworth'.** Photograph by Tony Wright, courtesy of *Railway Modeller*

We now have several tag strips spotted about the layout and another, larger tag strip on the control panel. These need to be methodically connected with more wire. The accepted practice is to connect one wire at a time and check that it is correct before moving on to the next. You now have another bunch of wires draped around the layout. The old approach was to screw an array of large hooks to the L girders and hook the wires through these.

We now have a neater alternative. The electrical section of your local DIY store has 2-metre lengths of white plastic troughs, complete with snap-on covers. Its purpose is to provide a neat cover for surface mains wiring but it is even better at holding a bunch of low voltage wires. This trough can be fixed to the bottom of the L girder with wooden supports, as shown in Figure 9/10.

The wires are laid loosely along the trough and hidden from sight with the covers. You'll have to cut these into shorter lengths to allow the wires to emerge at tag strip locations. Jumbling the wires together in this fashion may seem unprofessional, but it's the method used by prototype signal engineers. There's a lot to be said for following prototype practice.

CHAPTER 10

BUILDING CONSTRUCTION

Buildings, on a model railway, fall into two distinct groups, those inside and those outside the boundary fence. Clearly, the key railway structures are the important ones, the station offices, signal cabins, goods and locomotive sheds, together with the many smaller ancillary huts, relay cabins and suchlike fittings that are found close to the lineside. Although both ready assembled and kit-built versions are readily available, these do not pretend to do more than provide a few examples culled from the enormous variety of architectural styles adopted by the companies which built Britain's railways. British station architecture is a fascinating study in its own right, several large well-illustrated books have been published on the subject without doing more than dipping into it.

Yet before we look at buildings, there is an important lineside structure to discuss, the raised platform so characteristic of the British railway scene. Platforms vary considerably in detail, but four important characteristics are common to the majority. They are approximately 3 feet above rail level (12mm for 00) and the edge is 4ft 6in (20mm) from the centre line of the track on straights, this is increased on curves. The width is usually more than 12 feet (48mm) and no fixed obstruction is nearer that 6ft (24mm) from the edge. In exceptional circumstances the platform may narrow to 10ft (40mm) at the ends. Finally, the platform always ends with a ramp, this has been required by Government regulations for over a century.

Hornby provides ready-made platforms which serve the purpose but have toylike curves so they can fit more readily inside a train set oval. The Peco plastic platform system provides a more flexible approach, offering a self assembly variable width unit for use with Setrack and plain edging for other purposes. Each come with a choice of brick or stone finish.

Platform construction is not difficult, a popular method is shown in Figure 10/1. Stripwood sides are covered with a thin top, generally 3mm ply, hardboard or MDF

sheet. The only real difficulty is getting the right height of stripwood, it needs to be 13.5mm high and as the usual offering is only ½in (12.5mm) the only simple answer is to have a 1mm thick card underlay. Edging stones should be scribed along the edge of the top surface. Use a carpenter's marking gauge, or a home made substitute for the long groove and scribe the individual slabs with the help of a small square. 8mm wide x 10mm long is a good size, the more so since marking out is eased when you use a major division on your rule.

Although a limited number of basic buildings, primarily from Hornby, can be found in the larger High Street stores, this is the point where one needs to draw on the wider selection available at a good model shop. You should by now be familiar with some model railway magazines. Through advertisements and reviews, these will show the range of kits available but for convenience, your local model railway exhibition will be supported by the active dealers in your vicinity. It is a good idea to support these enterprising firms since they can supply useful advice as well as affording you the opportunity to view the product before you buy.

Even the best dealers would be hard put to stock examples of every building kit currently available. Much of the vast output from the Continental plastic kit manufacturers is only available in Britain from a handful of specialist suppliers and not every item illustrated in the full colour catalogues from Faller, Kibri, Volmer and the rest can be supplied from stock. Indeed, even on their home territory, it is difficult to locate some of the less popular items from these ranges.

The majority of readily available railway structure kits fall into the category of representative types which do provide the newcomer with the essential basics and may be used with confidence. Size is probably a more significant factor than exact prototype design. It is when we move into the second category of buildings that the design becomes of greater significance.

Non-railway structures have a very important part to play around a model railway, since in addition to suggesting sources of traffic for the railway, they can provide a clue to the area in which the model is set. Again, a good selection of kits is available.

Many British building kits are printed in full colour on card. Those printed on thin sheet require reinforcing with thicker card. Although the card cut out is often aimed at children, and cardboard is a base material for modelling in schools and on TV programmes, it is not an easy material to use. The building kits designed to be folded are particularly difficult, since you must first cut out precisely on the line, then fold exactly along the dotted line and, before you finish assembly, provide internal reinforcing to prevent the thin sides from bowing inwards.

In comparison, the plastic kit is a very straightforward proposition. All one need do is to detach the parts from the sprue, remove the small moulding pips and then assemble in the order shown on the instruction leaflet. The main thing to avoid is leaving your thumbprint on the walls, this happens when you over apply the adhesive.

Most quality kits now advise the use of a liquid cement or solvent rather than tube cement. Liquid cements are normally applied inside the joints with a fine brush after the parts are held together dry. However, it is permissible to brush a thin film over the joint faces before assembly, this softens the plastic sufficiently for the two parts to take hold, the application of a thin film of liquid cement (not solvent) to the inside of the joint completes the job.

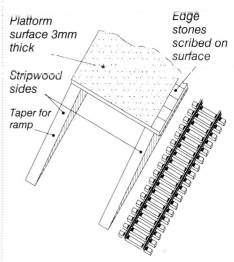

Platform surface 3mm thick

Edge stones scribed on surface

Stripwood sides

Taper for ramp

Figure 10/1: **Basic platform construction.**

Although liquid cement and solvents appear very similar, the former consists of the base solvent plus a modicum of plastic. Tube cement contains more plastic base. You can use pure solvent to thin down both tube cement and liquid cement, or make your own plastic cement by adding thin slivers of plastic to a small amount of solvent in a glass container. This is a tedious process and only recommended in emergencies.

Some liquid cements and most solvents come in tall, flat bottles which are easily tipped over. These can be fitted into a base, the favoured version being a piece of foam plastic, though for permanence the extra work needed to make the necessary hole in a piece of wood is well worthwhile. Best of all is to use a squat cylindrical or conical bottle and to decant the solvent into it.

Plastic cements and solvents give off toxic fumes and must only be used in a well-ventilated space. The problem of solvent abuse has restricted the availability of these useful materials and most shops will only sell these products to adults.

Although all but the cheapest of plastic building kits are 'self coloured', and can be assembled straight from the box, their appearance may be improved by judicious painting. For this purpose, acrylic paints are better than the usual oil-based 'model paints'. Acrylics have two distinct advantages. For a start, they do not have a gloss finish, highly undesirable on any model. Next, they have a water base. Not only does it come out of a tap at very low cost, it is the only safe solvent available, non-flammable, non-toxic and no fumes at room temperature. Its ready availability as a jet over the sink makes brush cleaning a joy.

Increasingly, acrylics are being used for model paints. Unless you need a small amount of a particular colour, the large tubes used by artists are more economical. You will need a palette onto which you squeeze small quantities of the colours and then mix to produce the required hue. The conventional oval artist's pattern has its value when painting landscapes, but for modelmaking a smaller glazed ceramic palette is best. Don't try to buy these in an artist's supplier, look instead for an old white saucer or a wall tile. These can be washed clean under a tap at the end of a painting session.

You need a good supply of brushes of varying sizes. Do not fall into the trap of purchasing a card of cheap brushes other than for rough work. For fine work, proper artist's watercolour brushes are best, they provide the fine point we need for the detailed application of paint. Moreover, brushes do wear, and after some time need to be downgraded to rougher work.

It is usually easier to paint most parts of a plastic kit before assembly. In particular, window frames, which are frequently separate mouldings, must be painted before insertion and the fitting of the glazing material.

An important technique for plastic kits, with their detail relief, is dry brushing. This is best tried out on a brick or stone pattern surface. An initial coat of 'mortar' colour is applied, this is generally a creamy yellow, but for old structures can be nearer black. When dry, the 'brick' colour is applied almost dry, the brush being lightly passed over the surface so that only the raised detail is covered. For brick, burnt sienna and yellow ochre are the base colours, these may be mixed together to provide different hues. The addition of a little red is needed for some new brickwork. A little experimentation will be needed, while as a guide a few close-up colour photos of local walls will be found invaluable.

The wide variety of building designs and styles on the prototype make this field the most fertile for scratchbuilding. A building is really no more than an assembly of different sized and shaped boxes, with holes cut out for windows, doors and other openings. Unfortunately, many of us were introduced to this idea at school, where we were encouraged to cut holes in cardboard boxes with a pair of scissors. Given sufficient practice a rough caricature of a building can be produced, but it is not the way to set about the task. Nor, for that matter, is it a good idea to make a cardboard carcass from a single sheet by cutting and folding. Leave that sort of thing to origami.

Whether you use card, wood or plastic sheet, the correct approach to model building construction is to make each wall a separate unit. The necessary openings are then cut into the flat sheet and, in most cases, the door and window frames, together with doors and glazing added while the sheet is flat. Once this is done, the sides are secured together. The best way to sum up the process is to say that scratchbuilding is a system of kit assembly where you begin by making the kit for yourself.

A small hut is the best starting point, it involves very few parts and a home can always be found for it on the layout. Figure 10/2 gives the sizes of the individual items, which are cut from 40 thou (1mm) thick plastic sheet. The door and window are shown in the same wall but if you prefer to have the door in an end wall, well, it's your model. The floor is optional, but helps

Isometric sketch of hut

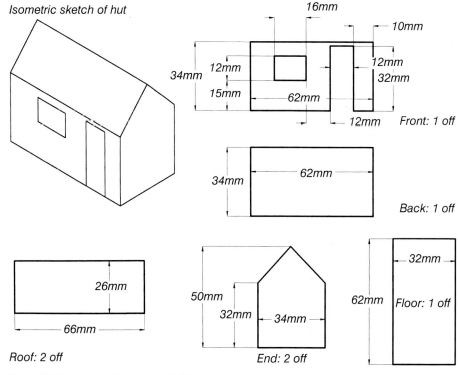

Figure 10/2: **Parts for a simple scratchbuilt hut.**

Figure 10/3: **Modelling doors by layers.**

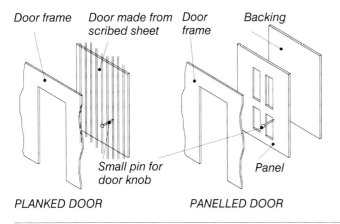

Door frame   Door made from scribed sheet   Door frame   Backing

Small pin for door knob   Panel

PLANKED DOOR   PANELLED DOOR

Figure 10/4: **Two approaches to window construction.**

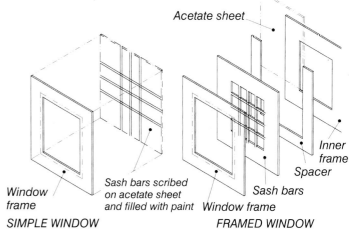

Acetate sheet

Inner frame
Spacer
Sash bars
Window frame
Window frame   Sash bars scribed on acetate sheet and filled with paint

SIMPLE WINDOW   FRAMED WINDOW

Figure 10/6: **Low relief construction for a small shop.**

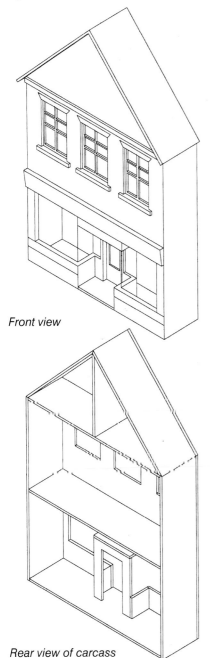

Front view

Rear view of carcass

Figure 10/5: **Analysis of a modern chalet bungalow model.**

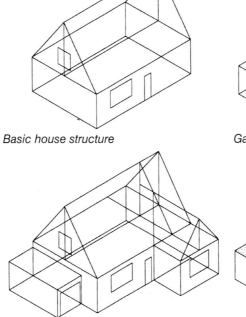

Basic house structure   Garage added

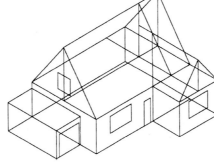

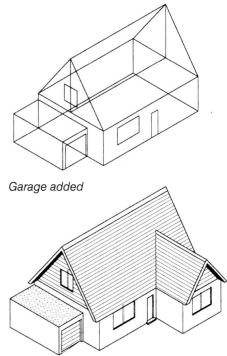

Extension added   Complete building

keep the structure square. No overall finish is suggested, you can apply brick paper or use thin embossed plastic sheet overlays.

If preferred, you can use card, but good quality thick card is not widely available and thin card tends to bow. You will need to adjust the sizes in this case. There is much to be said for using empty cereal packets for one's first attempts, the base material costs nothing but the card is of good quality and can be readily cut with a craft knife. This is best done on a plastic cutting board, these are self sealing and, although they do wear out in time, years of modelling can be done before both sides

are too far gone to be used. Apart from the knife and cutting board, you need a steel straightedge, a rule is the usual tool.

Plastic sheet is handled in the same manner as card, with one small difference, it is not always necessary to cut through the sheet. In most cases a half cut will allow the brittle sheet to be broken along the cutting line, but for intricate cuts it is usually best to cut through the material.

Plastic sheet is available in a number of thicknesses, these are normally given in thous ($\frac{1}{1000}$ in), the rating is nominal. As well as plain sheet, Slaters provide 20 thou Plastikard sheets, roughly A4 size, with a

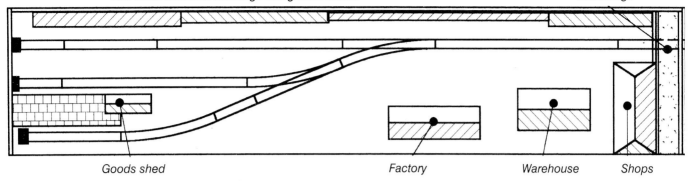

Low relief industrial buildings along back-scene   *Overbridge*

Goods shed   *Factory*   *Warehouse*   *Shops*

Figure 10/7: **'Highfield Yard' completed with low relief and solid buildings with an overbridge masking the exit.**

Top left: **Early stages in the construction of a plastic kit-based inn. One wall, complete with window frames, has been cemented to the base.**

Top right: **Although the base should help set the walls at a right angle it helps to check with a square. Here a small piece of brass which has been filed to a true square, with one corner relieved to clear the internal housings found on kit walls.**

Centre left: **The four walls have now been erected. It is a good idea at this point to leave the joints to harden before adding the annexe or the roof. It is very easy to break joints until the cement has had at least a couple of hours drying time.**

Centre right: **The completed inn, with roof and guttering added. The kit is finished, but the model requires added detail to bring it to life.**

Left: **A fine example of town modelling occupying very little space on a medium sized layout. The buildings are a combination of full models and low relief, neatly terraced to save space – as on the prototype. The break between back-scene painting and three dimensional model is hardly discernible from this angle.**

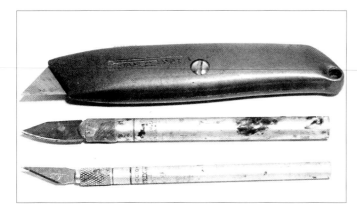

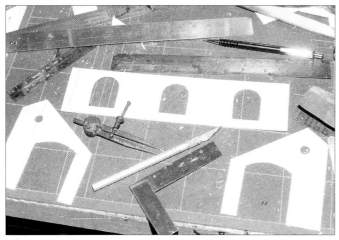

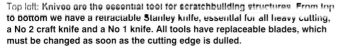

Top left: Knives are the essential tool for scratchbuilding structures. From top to bottom we have a retractable Stanley knife, essential for all heavy cutting, a No 2 craft knife and a No 1 knife. All tools have replaceable blades, which must be changed as soon as the cutting edge is dulled.

Centre left: Early stages in the construction of a scratchbuilt 4mm scale goods shed. The model is to go hard against the back-scene and is accordingly partially truncated at the back. Work is being carried out on a plastic cutting mat which is another invaluable adjunct to the modelmaker's tool-kit since, unlike the scrap material we used to have to employ, it does not get grooved as you cut through materials. The front wall and ends have been cut from 40 thou polystyrene sheet.

Bottom left: Scratchbuilding can be defined as a process of kit building where the modelmaker begins by making the kit. Here we see the main parts for the goods shed cut out ready for assembly. The walls have been covered with Slater's embossed brick sheet, layered to represent the piers and wider base. The arches are Ratio components. The window frames were cut out

from 20 thou plastic sheet, a tedious task. As there is some risk of breakage, four frames were marked out and cut so that in the event of trouble, there was a matching spare.

Top right: As there is no base to the building, it is essential to use a true square during assembly, in this instance an engineer's pattern 3in square. The end pier is not covered with brick sheet, since this will overlap the corner.

Centre right: Before too much work was carried out, the part assembled building was offered up onto the layout as a final check. As all the necessary measurements had been taken at the outset, and the parts set out carefully, this was more a reassurance exercise than a necessity.

Bottom right: The model is all but finished, the walls have been painted, as has the roof of the small office building. The roof has still to be attended to. The window frames were painted before assembly or glazing, this avoids any risk of getting the paint on the wrong parts.

Top left: **A row of low-relief industrial buildings to be set along a back scene. The Oblong Box Company is a very busy place, you will find their useful products everywhere. As their slogan has it, Oblong Boxes are Best.**

Top right: **Behind the scenes of the low-relief factories. The left hand windows are made from scribed acetate sheet, the right hand ones are commercial mouldings from Faller. These are no longer available, but British firms now supply a reasonable selection of moulded window frames.**

Left: **'Ingle Nook Sidings' goods shed, demonstrating that you can reduce size appreciably without losing character. Miniature railwaymen add life to the scene, but if that crate is to go into the back of the car, the rear springs are going to complain!**

wide variety of embossed patterns. Wills make a range of moulded sheets with varying textures, these are approximately 2mm thick and are fairly small. Both types may be intermixed, but the thinner Slaters material really needs to be applied as an overlay to a thicker base or else very liberally supported with internal bracing.

Doors and windows call for careful construction, more than anything else they provide the character of a building. Figures 10/3 and 10/4 show the basic methods of construction. Window glazing is normally acetate sheet, which has a tendency to bow over time and can fall out. The more elaborate assembly shown on the right of Figure 10/4 not only avoids any risk of this happening, it, in theory, allows the glazing to be removed for painting. The drawing shows separately cut glazing bars, but the simple scribed effect can be used if preferred.

Even the most complex buildings can be broken down into a series of little

boxes. Figure 10/5 shows how a typical modern chalet bungalow is built up from three units. However, you don't necessarily stick boxes onto the main structure. In this instance the forward projection forms part of the main structure, with the far wall forming a single unit. The garage could be an add on building, though the prototype on which this sketch is based has the rear walls flush. It also has a large dormer on the back roof. It is one of my former homes. Your own home is an ideal subject for your first attempt at a detailed model building, it's so easy to check details.

Low relief buildings are very popular as backdrops, they take up little room and, unlike the printed back-scene, do not look odd when viewed at an angle. The general principle is given in figure 10/6 which shows the front and rear of a model shop. The beauty of the low relief model is that you are only faced with detailing one wall, only in exceptional cases are the sides anything more than blank walls. These

structures resemble film and TV sets, you only model the bit that's seen, what goes on behind the scene is nobody's business, and is generally a maze of reinforcing struts. Figure 10/7 shows 'Highfield Yard' with the addition of buildings, most of which are low relief structures along the back-scene.

Building construction is a craft in its own right and has been the subject of many books. Most of those currently available deal with the more advanced levels of the craft, but do cover the essential basics as well. There is a lot to be said for the newcomer seeing how an expert sets about the task, but it is always advisable to remember that even the experts had to begin somewhere – and that their first efforts were frequently no better than your own initial attempts.

CHAPTER 11

THE FINISHING TOUCHES

We have now covered the fundamentals of model railway construction and have reached the point where the layout can be operated realistically and the main elements are present. We could stop there, but to do so would mean that we are ignoring one of the most enjoyable parts of the hobby.

At this point our model resembles one of those dummies used in staged crashes to determine what could happen to the people in the car were it for real. Just as the dummy is a recognisable caricature and appears to react as a human would, but is clearly a fake, so our model lacks the detail that makes it an individual creation. Adding these touches brings the railway to life.

The first feature that demands attention is the track, since it is without an essential part of the prototype, ballast. Unlike the full size railway, which uses ballast not only to provide drainage, but also to hold the sleepers in place, our ballast is a cosmetic feature. Foam ballast inlay is available, I've mentioned it earlier, but it isn't quite as easy to use as it looks - you must never pin the track down if you're to get good running - and it doesn't really look like stone chippings. Indeed the one thing that really does look like stone chippings is stone

chippings, but there are some plastic substitutes that come very close.

Loose ballasting is a convenient misnomer. The ballast is only loose when first applied. It is teased into shape with a flat brush and soaked with diluted PVC adhesive, about half and half glue and water. Some modellers first spray the ballast with 'wet water', which comes straight out of the tap, but has a drop of detergent added to reduce the surface tension. I add the detergent to the diluted PVA. Washing up liquid is the most readily available. You could use wetting agent, sold in all photographic stores, but as we're not working with critical chemical reagents, a spot of lemon essence substitute does no harm. PVA is transparent when dry; allow 24 hours for the ballast to harden. Some touching in will almost certainly be needed. Loose ballast does help hold the track in place, so it is best applied after you are satisfied with the track layout.

One important detail that should be high on your list of priorities is signalling. In full size, signals serve to provide a link between the signalmen and controllers on the lineside with the driver in the train. As a model railway operator, except on very large group operated layouts, combines all these functions, the primary purpose of

the signal does not exist. Hence many layouts remain unsignalled, despite the fact that the owner fully intends to install them – when he gets around to it.

Figure 11/1 shows the arrangement of British semaphore block signalling, along with the generally accepted designation of the signals. On most model railways we can ignore the distant signal, it is at least a quarter of a mile down the line, well outside the area being modelled. Indeed, we can soon discover that a lot of the closer signals are also offstage. 'Westleigh's signals are shown in Figure 11/2. There would also be a two-arm bracket signal controlling entry to the station, but this would be placed on the far side of the road bridge where the driver could see it clearly. Since it is outside the modelled area, we must ignore it, which is a pity since it is a very attractive feature.

Hornby list semaphore signals as accessories, they are typical British upper quadrant patterns and are robust rather than true to scale. More accurate models are provided by specialist concerns. Ratio offers a range of plastic upper and lower quadrant signals and kits – lower quadrants were in later years solely found on the Western Region. Model Railway Signal Engineering have a much larger selection of metal components and kits and publish a general guide to the subject.

Often, semaphore signals are there to look pretty and do not work. Figure 11/3 shows that a simple push rod actuated mechanism, incorporating a bell crank, can give life to the scene. The two stop pins protect the relatively delicate signal operating wire from damage.

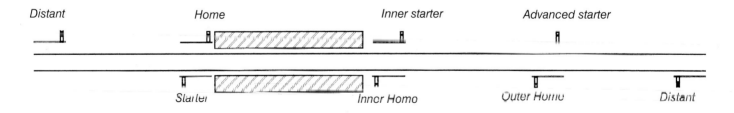

Figure 11/1: **Basic semaphore signal positions for block working.**

Figure 11/2: **Signal locations for 'Westleigh'. The two signals on the left will only be needed when the stone yard extension is built.**

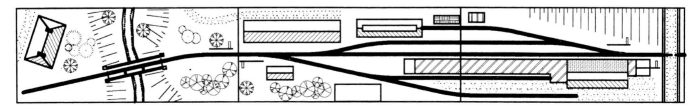

Above: **This 3-arm bracket signal was constructed from Ratio scale signal kits, even though, officially, they don't make this pattern of signal. It called for a little ingenuity, adding an extra bracket to the standard two-arm version.**

Figure 11/3: **Operating an upper quadrant semaphore signal by a push rod.**

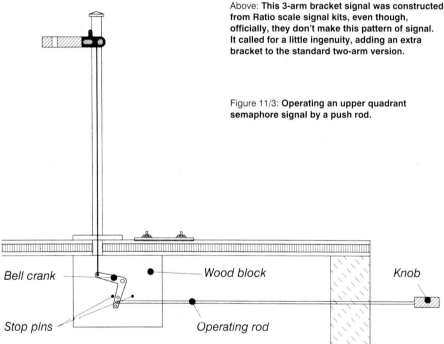

Colour light signals are easier to make work, though the moment you advance from the simple two aspect (red and green) signal which is a straightforward replacement for the semaphore to multiple aspect signalling the wiring can get complicated. Fortunately single track lines are commonly equipped with two aspect signals, so 'Avon' presents little difficulty. A simple two way switch is needed to change from green to red and vice versa.

Another important feature is street and station lamps. These are easier to arrange though again there is the sneaking feeling that they ought to work. There is much to be said for providing full illumination on a model scene, provided it is possible to view the model in near darkness. There also is the important consideration that it is a task that cannot be partially undertaken, because gaps in the lighting scheme are all too obvious. In particular, full train lighting is essential and that is not for the faint hearted.

Platform lamps lead us to the rest of the platform furniture, seats, poster boards, trolleys and luggage. The danger here is overloading the model, the more so since platforms on most model railways are much narrower than on the prototype, as well as being significantly shorter. Remember there must be room for the passengers.

Which brings us to the various characters that should populate your model world. The last thirty years have seen a transformation in this area, prior to this only a limited selection of figures, frequently in wooden poses, were available. Today there is an excellent selection on the market. Hornby and Peco offer a useful selection for the newcomer, ready painted and covering the major categories, station staff and passengers. A word of warning, some, whilst striking attractive poses, are not altogether suitable. A good example of this is the guard, who stands holding his flag to advise the driver that the train is ready to depart. Unfortunately, he remains there, still holding the flag, long after the train has left the station. Most aspects of railway operation can be simulated, one that is unlikely ever to be mastered is the business of getting people on and off the trains.

The largest range of miniature figures is provided by the German firm, Preiser. Their characters are available in most modelling scales *except* 4mm to the foot. This is largely because there is no great demand for this as British modellers are happy to use their HO models. Provided one does not mix HO and 00 figures, all is well. Preiser not only supply painted sets, but include boxes of unpainted figures which are excellent value for money. Painting miniature figures calls for a fine brush, a steady hand and an illuminated magnifying glass so that you can see what you are doing. Acrylic paints are ideal for this job.

Cast whitemetal figures in 4mm scale are provided by several firms. The major supplier is Langley Models, who also provide a host of other scenic features, including formed plastic low relief kits, which demand skilled painting, and an ever growing range of road vehicles.

The selection of detailing components and scenic accessories now available for the small scale railway modeller is vast and I have only touched on the more obvious fittings and mentioned long established manufacturers who are likely to be around for many years to come. There are many more firms providing these parts and even the largest model railway retailer simply cannot stock the lot, let alone find space to display small items which need to be seen to be appreciated. Specialist suppliers are often to be found at the larger model railway exhibitions. There is one simple rule to apply, when you see something you think you might want at an exhibition, buy it there and then. Otherwise you may have to wait a year for another chance, provided the firm in question still thinks it worthwhile attending, or is still in business. Remember, the finest model, kit or component on the market is of no use gathering dust in the manufacturer's stockroom or even languishing on a dealer's shelf. Only when it is in a modelmaker's possession can its potential be realised.

Top right: **This-kit built Continental farm has been embellished with additional detail in the farmyard and a poster on the gate. The various items dotted about add life to the model.**

Centre left: **Cast whitemetal station personnel. These figures not only need painting, it will be necessary to remove them from their 'concrete slabs'. This error is rarely perpetuated in current figure production – the base is only suited to toy usage, even wargamers assemble groups of figures on sub-bases so they can be readily moved into battle as a proper unit.**

Centre right: **The largest range of human figures in the biggest selection of scales is provided by the German firm, Preiser. Considerable attention is paid to providing character. Some twenty years ago they introduced a set of 'heads of state', all instantly recognisable. With the passage of time, only two of the group survive in office. Another set, TV and cine cameraman complements the heads of state.**

Above right: **A British range of service personnel. There are actually three sets shown, as other than in wartime it is unlikely one would see all three services so lavishly represented at any station. The transparent bases are readily removed.**

Right: **Passengers, staff and scavengers on Bob Harper's 7mm scale 'Maristow', a model set around the turn of the century. Note the waiting luggage – very important in Edwardian days – and the many enamelled iron advertisements fixed to the wooden fence.**

CHAPTER 12

STOCK AND OPERATION

Well before the construction of your model railway is complete, you will have been thinking about adding to the rolling stock you assembled at the start for the test train. In all probability you will have already started collecting the stud that will operate the finished model, if indeed any model railway can be regarded as being finished.

While the test train can be made up of anything that will run, the locomotives, coaches and wagons you amass for the line's operation should ideally form a coherent, logical collection. As this is a far from ideal world, it is more than likely that you will include some items which may be 'out of place' but are personal favourites. The only logical argument against this widespread practice is financial, if you can afford to add a model that doesn't fit into your overall design, well, that's one of life's little luxuries you should never deny yourself.

As you develop the layout from the bare baseboards you should have been thinking about the two key factors in ultimate realism, where and when. Indeed, there are those who maintain that these twin decisions ought to be made before you even put pencil to paper to plan the model. This is easy enough for an experienced railway modeller embarking on his or her third or later layout. The newcomer is unlikely to have the detailed knowledge needed to make an informed choice. While one can make an arbitrary decision on inadequate data, it is not a good idea when, as in this case, the choice may be deferred. Many layouts have changed course part way through construction.

Although the general locale of the model is to some extent set by the buildings, the locomotives and rolling stock are the key players in the drama. Since they are not fixed to the infrastructure, it is easy to use them to fine tune the model. So, by the time you begin assembling the stud in earnest you should have some idea of the period and prototype you want to follow. The date of the model is, today, the prime consideration since for most of the past half century, all British railways have been under the one umbrella, the nationalised system. When the target decade has been decided upon, you can begin to eliminate those locomotives, coaches and wagons that fall outside this period. From there you narrow down the choice to reflect the traffic pattern appropriate to your model.

Although the construction of a model railway is a satisfying project in its own right, we must never forget that the ultimate aim of the hobby is to operate small scale trains in a convincing setting in accordance with full sized practice. Indeed, the real difference between a fully developed train set and a model railway is that you can only play with the train set, whereas you can also, on a model railway, run your own miniature transport system. You can also play trains as well when the mood takes you.

With a couple of exceptions it is possible to mimic the detailed operation of a full sized railway to a small scale. The most important piece of equipment you need for this is your own ingenuity and imagination. The main tools are pencil, pen and paper, these remain the traditional mainstay of full-size timetable offices despite the existence of computers.

Where a computer is available, it can be used to produce neat and authentic looking printouts of both timetables and other operating documents and reduce the reams of easily jumbled paper to a collection of ordered files on a floppy disk. To generate a timetable by computer calls for considerable experience with spreadsheets and a detailed knowledge of prototype timetable generation. Full size railways use highly specialised software which can take a team of experienced programmers over a year to develop and a further six months to debug. Happily, the less complicated model railway doesn't need anything like this degree of sophistication.

Although we think initially of timetables, on all but the most elaborate of model railways we do not need to get involved with time, let alone the complications of speeded clocks. Instead, we have a schedule which gives the order of train movements which are generally numbered for convenience. These movements may be worked out in advance, this is an exercise that can make good use of time spent commuting to work by public transport. It is equally possible to do this empirically, by operating the railway and recording your moves as you go along. In practice, most schedules, full size or model, are produced by a combination of theory and practice, where the initial paper-based scheme is modified in the light of experience.

All operating schedules are, in essence, cyclical. At the end of the working cycle, generally a complete day, everything should be back where it started. On a full sized railway this is rarely possible, stock gets out of place for a variety of reasons. On a model railway one can achieve the ideal because there are far fewer elements involved and the only chance occurrence that can upset the pattern is the mechanical failure of one or more items of rolling stock. Even then, order can be restored by lifting the offending vehicle off the track and replacing it with a spare, one point where we have a distinct advantage over the full size operator.

It is a good idea to prepare a list showing where the stock should be at the start of operation, generally 00:00 hours (midnight). Taking, for our example, 'Westleigh' in its basic form, this will detail the two trains in the fiddle yard, the locomotive in the shed and the location of any stock that is left overnight in the station. Assuming a steam age GWR setting, a 14xx 0-4-2 tank would be in the shed and its trailer coach would be standing on the shunting spur. Two of the three fiddle yard sidings would be occupied by a goods train headed by an 0-6-0 pannier tank and a passenger train hauled by a 2-6-2 tank, the third would be vacant. A selection of goods wagons would be in the sidings.

The next moves could follow the pattern below.

1   14xx comes off shed and couples onto trailer coach; moves into platform to form push-pull train.
2   Push-pull train departs for fiddle yard.
3   Locomotive hauled passenger train leaves fiddle yard for platform.
4   2-6-2 tank uncouples from train and pulls forward onto shunting neck.
5   2-6-2 tank reverses around train via the loop, onto track 1 of fiddle yard.
6   2-6-2 tank backs onto train and couples up.

7 Goods train arrives behind 0-6-0 tank on loop road, detaches brake van.

8 2-6-2 and train return to fiddle yard.

9 Push pull arrives from fiddle yard.

10 Goods train, less brake van moves onto shunting spur.

11 Push pull departs for fiddle yard.

12 0-6-0 tank pushes goods train into platform road, uncouples and reverses onto shunting spur.

13 0-6-0 tank moves onto loop and couples to brake van.

14 0-6-0 tank and brake van moves onto shunting spur.

15 0-6-0 tank and brake van couples to goods train in platform road.

16 0-6-0 tank and reformed goods train move onto shunting spur.

17 2-6-2 tank and train arrive at platform.

18 0-6-0 tank shunts sufficient wagons into goods yard to allow room on spur for the 2-6-2 tank.

19 2-6-2 tank runs round train as moves 4 to 6. Goods stock is also shunted to form new train.

20 2-6-2 tank and train depart for fiddle yard.

21 New goods train backed into loop, locomotive runs round and couples to front.

22 Push-pull arrives from fiddle yard.

23 Goods train departs to fiddle yard.

I have repeatedly used the term 'run round the train'. To experienced workers this is self-evident but newcomers will not be familiar with the term, nor will they have ever seen it performed other than on a preserved line or a layout at an exhibition. Figure 12/1 shows the sequence of events at 'Westleigh'.

These moves only take us to mid morning. A similar pattern of moves can continue through the model day. At the end the push pull arrives, deposits its coach on the spur and then goes onto shed, leaving everything where it began. The cycle can then restart, you can operate a different schedule or you can, in the fullest sense of the phrase, call it a day and pack everything away.

Clearly, the addition of the stone yard extension will call for another goods train. As this will fill all three fiddle yard roads, you have first to clear a track for the push-pull, which means that one of the two goods trains has to run into the loop as move 2. The push-pull then departs, allowing the goods locomotive to run round the train and propel it to the stone yard. This shows that although a three-track fiddle yard is fine at the outset, four or five tracks are a better proposition. It is not unduly difficult to make a larger sector plate when you feel it is necessary since all you need do is remove one screw and detach one wire to remove the old one.

While all these moves can be typed out onto an A4 sheet, most operators prefer to transfer the information to flip cards. These are a series of numbered cards listing the various moves in detail, provided with a pair of punched holes at the top of each card. The cards are threaded onto the twin clips of a ring binder. Unfortunately, these are not easily available except as part of a complete binder. Even if a battered binder is not available, dismantling a new binder does leave you with two reasonable sized pieces of stiff card and the modelmaker who cannot find a use for these has yet to be found. The rivets need to be drilled out, leaving holes for the screws holding the clip to a convenient surface. Figure 12/2 shows the basic set-up, the active card will be seen to be part of the sequence above.

The cards are standard office filing cards, the smallest pattern is generally sufficient for our needs. The holes are produced with a standard office punch. It might be found convenient to fit a simple gauge to an old punch to ensure that all cards have their holes in the same place. This makes for a neater appearance.

For added realism, you can allocate arrival and departure times, but these are notional. In other words, when the 8:15 local service leaves, it is 8:15. If the next arrival is scheduled for 8:55, then the moment it stops at the platform it is 8:55. That, in real time, just over a minute will have elapsed is immaterial. Editing out the long wait between trains makes for more interesting operation. Indeed, at a public exhibition, the better organised operators ensure that there is always something happening on the visible part of the layout.

We have only considered the bare bones of the schedule. Considerable refinement is possible, either by tweaking the initial scheme or by the natural growth of the locomotive stud and the rolling stock roster. Another refinement is to create a background story to the layout. This is where modelling an actual prototype station places an unnecessary limitation on the layout development, since the background is fixed and hence the traffic pattern effectively frozen. With an imaginary prototype, the scope is only limited by your own imagination. You can create a complete community peopled with characters of your own choice. They don't need to behave rationally, though it is best that there should be an underlying logic, no matter how weird it might be.

Although it is customary to set a model railway in a known background, usually in one's own native land, you aren't at all constrained. You could never see the full size Flying Scotsman headed by a Gresley A3 pass the Orient Express hauled by a Chapelon Pacific, for all that both trains ran in the same era. You can stage this scene on a model railway despite the fact that although both names survive, the trains have altered out of all recognition.

You can also have models of the Flying Scotsman as it appeared down the years. You will need at least six different trains merely to represent the best known versions, six wheelers behind a Stirling Single, East Coast Joint stock behind an Ivatt Atlantic, LNER teak carriages with a Gresley A3, BR Mark 1 coaches and an A4 pacific, a Deltic with Mark 2 coaches and finally a Class 90 electric locomotive with Mark 4 coaches. Even if your layout is no more than the Welwyn Viaduct backed by a set of storage sidings you'll have an exciting model.

The practice of using a novel, or series of novels to form the background of your railway is well established. If you wish to model the Ruritanian State Railway, go ahead. You won't get much help from the novels, they merely report that there were trains. This is not necessarily a disadvantage, you can decide how they looked and where the tracks ran and no-one can argue otherwise.

Of course, if two people decided to model Ruritania, it is probable that two different versions will emerge. Since what you do on your layout has no effect on what anybody else does on theirs, this is of no account whatsoever. It has been said that building a model railway means creating a little world where you don't have to live. This is true, it also means you have a world where you can exclude anybody you don't like for any reason you think fit and where everything runs as you think it should. In a way, that is what railway modelling is really about.

Operating a model railway in a purposeful manner, simulating so far as possible the working of a full size railway is the best way of sustaining interest in the model over a period of years. It is also a means of deciding on future developments, either through adding extra sidings or even platforms to cope with increased traffic – always provided there is room to do this. However, it should never be regarded as the be-all and end-all of train operation. The majority of railway modellers do, from time to time, 'play trains', in other words, run trains haphazardly as the whim takes them. Often this is described as 'test running', which gives the process a veneer of respectability, since grown men do not indulge in childish practices. Mind you, some people do carry out a lot of tests. The important point to bear in mind is that it is your railway and you must run it as you see fit.

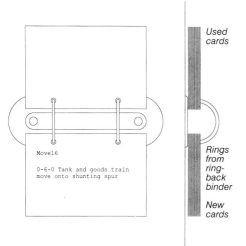

Figure 12/2: **One of the movement cards for the 'Westleigh' layout, as discussed on page 55.**

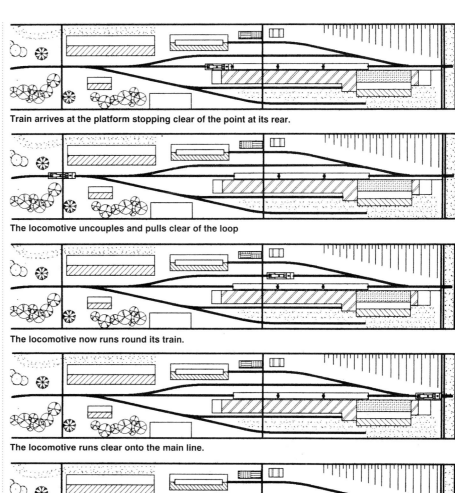

Train arrives at the platform stopping clear of the point at its rear.

The locomotive uncouples and pulls clear of the loop

The locomotive now runs round its train.

The locomotive runs clear onto the main line.

Finally the locomotive pulls forward onto its train and couples up to leave bunker first.   Figure 12/1

Right: **During the steam age, goods were delivered by rail in a wide variety of wagons. Although straightforward open trucks and closed vans predominated, they came in many guises as this very typical between the wars goods yard scene reveals.**

CHAPTER 13

THE DIESEL ERA

In the mid 1960s, Sydney Pritchard and I coined the term 'Modern Image' to describe the new railway system coming into being in Britain. Our object was to counter the common attitude of the time when enthusiasts talked of 'boxes on wheels' – and that was when they were being polite.

To our delight, the term caught the public's attention and it is now used to describe any model railway using diesel or electric outline traction. Since a model based on 1970s practice is as much an historical statement as any steam age layout, I now prefer to speak of the diesel era before getting down to defining exactly when, in that period – already more than 30 years in extent – the model is based.

Although the term apparently excludes electric traction, the absence of a ready-to-run British electric multiple unit set and British overhead catenary systems makes this aspect of the railway scene less attractive to the beginner. That the problems are far from insuperable is undeniable, but at present the beginner is best advised to look on this as a long-term possibility.

Most forms of diesel traction, and examples of modern passenger and freight stock are widely available. For most newcomers they will be the first and most obvious choice. How well do they fit the layouts described in this book?

'Avon' is best worked by modern traction, as mentioned a the text. The simplified track layout and lack of locomotive handling sidings would make steam operation less realistic.

'Westleigh', on the face of it, is a steamage branch, but the introduction of the stone loading sidings offers a reason for its retention in the current railway scene. Such branches still exist.

Although 'Highfield Yard' appears to be the sort of installation swept away by modernisation, the fact is that the first use of diesel power in Britain was in goods yards, where six-coupled diesel mechanical shunters appeared in the 1930s. Moreover, the addition of a hopper loading plant could transform it into Highfield Roadstone PLC for the simple ladder formation is the favoured one for bulk loading.

The fact is that modern motive power is better suited to the beginner than steam outline models. For a start, the leading and trailing wheels on steam locomotives do derail on occasions, while the need to turn tender engines adds other problems. A turntable takes up a lot of room and can be a very costly item into the bargain.

From the outset, diesel and electric locomotives in Europe and the UK have been double ended, so do not require turning. Furthermore, all but the smallest diesel locomotives, used mainly for shunting, run on bogies. In model form, this produces a machine which will traverse sharp curves without looking ungainly, and rides better than a comparable steam outline model. Finally, there is the added advantage that, unlike steam locomotives, which were built as express passenger, mixed traffic and freight types, the modern diesel electric locomotive is equally at home on any type of train. It is somewhat ironic that, shortly after locomotive engineers delivered the universal machine that the operating staff had long required, management decided to sectorise and so segregate the locomotive stock.

The diesel railcar first appeared on British metals in the 1930s when the GWR introduced single unit streamlined cars on secondary main line services. These machines proved successful in generating new traffic and were followed by a production series of more angular vehicles which are available in model form from Lima. British Railways diesel multiple units (DMU) appeared in the 1950s as two- and three-car units and were widely used on secondary and branch line services well before main line diesel locomotives appeared in any noticeable numbers. Once again these early designs are available in model form. Today the modern DMU is widespread and the latest designs are readily available in model form.

In addition, the HST sets, with their fixed formations and power cars at each end are technically DMUs. Available as models, they have only one small blemish from the modeller's viewpoint, with seven or eight long coaches sandwiched between the two power cars, an accurate model of the train takes up a lot of room. The usual train set offering is somewhat over engined, but many modellers are content with a four coach set comprising one first, one buffet and two standard class coaches. This does present the spirit of the prototype but even so requires a good deal of space.

Loco-hauled passenger trains are more flexible, and although these are now being phased out on the prototype, it is unlikely they will disappear from model tracks.

Left: **The modern image railway reflecting an urban landscape provides as much scope for 'landscape' treatment as its rural equivalent. A popular 4mm scale exponent of the art is 'Hayley Mills' built by John and Steve Emerson. The staff at Soho Motors seem oblivious to the fact that 37 423** *Sir Murray Morrison* **is passing overhead with a ballast cleaner!** Photograph by Tony Wright, courtesy of British Railway Modelling

But before we consider the historic potential of the diesel era, two of its special attractions for the railway modeller need to be considered.

The first is the process of rationalisation, which has taken two forms, the reduction in numbers of tracks and sidings and the widespread use of block trains. This practice was followed by railway modellers from the earliest days and although the simplification of track formations was largely dictated by lack of space, block trains and permanently coupled sets of coaches were used on the model to reduce manpower requirements and improve operating efficiency. In this respect the prototype has apparently followed the model!

Another very important advantage of diesel era modelling is that the necessary research needed to create a convincing model can be carried out in the most enjoyable and convenient way, by direct observation. Although the reduction in the network has meant that, in many parts of Britain, one has to travel some distance to find a railway, it is still much easier to head to your nearest rail centre than it is to search through the local library for the details you require. For a start, no public library carries more than a fraction of the titles available and, even in a well stocked specialist library, you can spend hours searching in vain for a specific feature. On the prototype it is all there, spread out for your information.

Although it is still good fun to stand by the lineside and watch the trains go by, collection of prototype information for modelling purposes is best done in an organised manner. For a start you need comfortable clothing which has to be suited to the weather. The much derided anorak is popular precisely because it not only keeps out all but the worst the weather can throw at you, it has plenty of capacious pockets. I prefer a shoulder bag, since one really needs a large notepad, as well as a camera, whilst a packet of sandwiches and a litre bottle of soft drink take up a fair amount of space.

It is impossible to over-emphasize the value of a camera, equally it is all too easy to over specify the equipment needed. While a single lens reflex camera and a battery of lenses is, in expert hands, absolutely invaluable, a modern extended zoom compact camera is fully adequate for the job and weighs a great deal less. At the same time, the speed, flexibility and cost of modern colour print film allows one

Above: **The everyday clutter of modern day life contributes to the realism of this view of the 00 gauge layout 'Hayley Mills'. 60 084** *Cross Fell* **shows the superiority of rail transport over road!** Photograph by Tony Wright, courtesy of British Railway Modelling

to take plenty of photographs, while one can easily order large sized prints.

It is advisable to take a note of where and when you took the photos and to store the negatives carefully. Even though your records of the current scene might appear commonplace now, the situation will be radically different in 50 years time. I speak from personal experience.

Before I explore the implication of this, I should mention two recent developments, the Advance Photographic System and Digital Photography. The latter is still being developed, it is at present very costly and even its proponents admit that picture quality is far short of conventional film. In addition, the number of images one can economically take before downloading is limited. APS uses conventional film in an unconventional manner and has one serious fault at the time of writing, cost. Furthermore, the storage system, with the film in a bulky cassette, appears to pose considerable problems.

Good record photographs in time acquire archival status since even if the structure survives, it has frequently changed, in detail, if nothing else. It is not always appreciated just how rapid change can be. While this book was being written, the

appearance of the rolling stock on Britain's railways was undergoing a considerable change. As a result of privatization the ownership of the stock transferred to leasing companies, who in turn passed it on to be used by the actual TOCs (train operating companies). Most of these began to quickly stamp their own logos and liveries on the stock they used. Although these changes are only cosmetic, they will clearly have to be reflected in future models of Britain's railways in the later half of the 1990s. These are only the latest in a series of livery changes during the diesel era, but they are probably the most significant.

There are other, more subtle changes, both to the railway system itself and to the surrounding urban scene. Even the countryside changes. So, when you see any feature you think would make a good model, take a photograph as soon as you can. If you don't, someone will make a drastic change and spoil the effect.

Although we will not see any dramatic changes on the stroke of midnight on 31st December 1999, there is no doubt that as we move into the 21st century, more things will change and, what is more, will not alter in any predictable fashion. At least, they haven't done so to date. But change they will, and I confidently predict that anyone who takes pains to faithfully model the late 20th century scene will discover that, by 2010, his model is an historical record of a past era. One of the major reasons why established railway modellers appear to be working in the past is because, sooner

tendency today is to use block trains rather than individual wagons, there is still a reasonable amount of shunting potential.

Apart from this, some secondary routes were operated by loco-hauled trains until comparatively recently. Many of the northern Scottish routes were worked by three coach rakes of Mk1 coaches, hauled by a Class 37 diesel.

As a complete contrast, 'Avon' is best operated as a diesel era system, certainly the branch line can only be worked by railcars since no run round facilities exist. There is no branch platform either, so the basic operating pattern would be for the branch train to arrive first, then move off into the siding to clear the platform for a main line train. When the main line trains have passed and departed, the railcar would then return to the platform before departing up the branch. This creates a lot of movement around what is essentially a very simple station, whilst the business of stabling spare trains in the sidings adds further to the operating potential. In keeping with modern practice, freight would consist of block trains which would be parked, complete with their locomotives, in a siding when not running round the layout. Whether main line passenger services are worked by loco-hauled stock, railcars or very much shortened HST sets, is a matter for personal taste.

The best answer is to have them all, and to go one stage further, install overhead wiring and have electric stock as well. Obviously, with the limited storage capacity of the layout, you can't have them all on the layout at once, but since trains are not fixed items – this would defeat the object of the hobby – removing and replacing stock from time to time is a straightforward exercise. It calls for a degree of organisation, ranging from a simple shelving system on which the spare stock stands, preferably in the manufacturers boxes, to a partitioned drawer unit in which the models are resting on foam plastic. Such units exist, you find them in office suppliers as filing/stationary units, but the steel drawers are just deep enough to hold 00 rolling stock.

or later, there comes a time when trying to keep pace with prototype change is more trouble than it is worth.

It can indeed, be self defeating. An old friend set out to model an interesting secondary route with reasonable fidelity. It was a simple project, he soon had everything reproduced to his satisfaction, but by keeping abreast of the changes to the prototype, he sustained interest for some 20 years. Then, one day, they closed the line. Somehow, he just couldn't carry on.

For a diesel era model, the operating pattern of 'Westleigh' would be simplified, since such passenger services as did exist would be operated by a diesel railcar and the complex procedure for running round the train would not be necessary. While this simplifies matters considerably, it removes much of the fun from operation and to use railcars as the core traffic would rapidly lead to boredom.

This is why branch line modelling was, for many years, considered to be rooted in the steam age, but apart from the undeniable fact that the diesel era was ushered in by the wholesale closure of rural branch lines, the idea is invalid. Such branches as remain are predominately freight oriented, normally for mineral traffic, but any industry which makes a heavy use of rail traffic can be served. This is the reason for the stone siding on the branch, it brings the model into modern times. Although the

Top: **On Steve Adcock's 00 gauge 'Russell Bridge' a brace of Class 31s are in charge of the nuclear flask traffic, as a passenger service flashes by.** Tony Wright, courtesy of *British Railway Modelling*

Above: **Down by the riverside, English Electric Type 1 (later Class 20) D8046 arrives at 'Melbridge Dock', a small space 4mm scale exhibition layout constructed by Brian and Philip Parker.** Tony Wright, courtesy of *British Railway Modelling*

CHAPTER 14

WHERE DO WE GO FROM HERE?

We have now covered the basic principles of model railway construction and operation. There is no great need to go any further – many layouts featured in magazines and which appear regularly at model railway exhibitions delve no further into the hobby than this.

However, human nature being what it is, there will probably come a time when you will want to progress as your modelling skills improve. The choice of different periods and prototypes will loom large, but the over-riding factor will be the amount of space available for your new layout.

This brings the question of the different scales and gauges to the fore, but first go along and visit your local model shop to get a better idea of the 'look and feel' of the various scales and gauges, whether produced commercially, for which there will be a fair range of ready-to-run locos, rolling stock, track, buildings, kits and accessories available, or if not, it will be a matter of kitbuilding or scratch-building your own locomotives and rolling stock .

Here is a summary of the main choices, beginning with those which, through historical accident, are classed as 'standard gauge' and based on a 4ft 8½in prototype:

Above: **N gauge lends itself to sweeping scenic effects in a reasonable space. This is exemplified by the Chester Area N Gauge Group's superb model of Midford station on the former Somerset and Dorset Railway. This photo shows the viaduct and the end of the line's double track, where it passes over the former GWR branch to Limpley Stoke. This particular setting was used for the opening shots of the famous Ealing comedy 'The Titfield Thunderbolt', the railway scenes of which were filmed on the old GWR branch. The model recalls the flavour of these two lines, both of which have long been closed.**

STANDARD GAUGE

00 Gauge
**4mm to 1ft, 1:76 scale,
16.5mm gauge (inside track width)**
You may choose to continue with the scale and gauge that has been used for the projects featured in this book. Specifically a British system, this scale/gauge combination is very well provided for, with a plethora of ready-to-run models, kits and accessories. Although for historical reasons it suffers from a track gauge that is approximately 15% under scale (18.83mm would be correct) this remains a most popular format for those modelling British railways, from the 1923 Grouping period through to the present diesel and electric systems.

Having looked at the gauge which you will now be familiar with, here are the other 'standard gauge' options, beginning with the larger models:

1 Gauge
**10mm to 1ft, 1:30.5 scale
1¾in (44.45mm) gauge (track width)**
This scale, is nearly the biggest used for standard gauge (and narrow gauge) models. Some modellers prefer to use ⅜in to 1ft which gives a more accurate scale/gauge ratio and makes scaling from prototype drawings easier. Unless there are no budgetary constraints, most of the models would have to be scratch-built, although Gauge 1 does have some commercial support in Continental Europe, and some very fine, but extremely expensive, Continental and British-outline ready-to-run live steam or electric models are available. Peco and Tenmille Products produce track and the latter also offers a range of reasonably priced wagon and coach kits. A few locomotive and wagon kits are beginning to appear from some British manufacturers to cater for the growing interest in this scale. Support is available through the Gauge 1 Association, membership of which is essential if you expect to make any significant progress.

0 Gauge
**7mm to 1ft, 1:43.5 scale
32mm gauge (inside track width)**
0 gauge is on the borderline between commercial and non-commercial. Although once regarded as the preserve of those modellers with the necessary engineering skills to scratch-build, it has seen considerable growth in popularity in recent years, mainly due to the availability of a large range of good quality locomotive and rolling stock kits (in white-metal, photo-etched brass and/or nickel-silver, or resin-cast with etched brass components) that will build into highly detailed models. These kits (and a range of accessories) can be obtained by visiting certain model shops, by mail-order from the latter or direct from the manufacturer concerned.

There are at present two ways of acquiring ready-to-run locomotives and rolling stock. The first is to contact one of the many individuals willing to either scratch-build or assemble a commercially produced kit of either a locomotive or item of rolling stock. The second way is to buy one of the few injection-moulded plastic or resin-cast locomotives that are on the market. The latter are available only by mail-order.

There are two truly minor anomalies: the scale is nearly always quoted as 1:43, but in true mathematical terms is 1:43.5 – and the inside track gauge width of 32mm is a touch under scale by nearly a millimetre – it should really be 32.958 – an error of 3%: but see ScaleSeven below.

Anyone who wants to become involved in 7mm scale modelling would be well advised to join the Gauge 0 Guild Ltd, the address of which will be available at your local model shop. The Guild produce an A4 quarterly magazine containing useful articles and all the answers to the availability of 7mm products and services.

ScaleSeven
**7mm to 1ft, 1:43.5 scale
32.95mm gauge (inside track width)**
This relatively new refinement involves the use of exact scale wheel profiles and an exact scale/gauge ratio, which gives a slight increase in track width (from the commercially accepted 32mm) to give even greater accuracy.

Above: **0 gauge 7mm scale LNER K3 hauls a passenger express on the layout of Maurice Nagington.** Photograph by Tony Wright

S Gauge
³⁄₁₆ in (4.76mm) to 1ft, 1:64 scale
22.2mm (⅞ in) gauge (track width)
The name was derived from the 'S' in Seven-eighths and in one Sixty-fourth. It has been established for many years, and essential parts can be obtained from the S-Gauge Society. A few locomotive and wagon kits were produced in Britain, but there is little or no commercial support other than in the USA. It enjoys a near perfect scale/gauge ratio and falling between 0 and 00, it provides scope for detailing without occupying a lot more space than 00. The modeller in this gauge must expect to have to scratch-build or adapt almost everything, but very high standards have been achieved, as witnessed in the modelling press and at exhibitions.

EM gauge
4mm to 1ft, 1:76 scale
18.2mm gauge (inside track width)
Anyone who has bothered to do a little arithmetic will realise that the 16.5mm of 00's track gauge only represents a full size measurement of 4ft 1In – no less than 7½ inches under size.

In an attempt to make the 00 layout track gauge look more realistic, combined with a desire to use the same wheel standards as 00, the 'EM' (Eighteen Millimetre) gauge, came about. A subsequent revision of the wheel and track standards prompted a track gauge adjustment to 18.2mm. Although this still fell short of the ideal (18.83mm) it was felt by those involved to be near enough.

Easy to assemble track is available from Ratio in 18.2mm gauge. Ready-made track is available from one or two sources or can be made up using components from Peco or other manufacturers.

In practice, the usual procedure has been to fit new wheel sets. The latter can be supplied by the EM Society, which also provides excellent support, and their loose-leaf manual covers all the practical points needed for success in this size.

P4 gauge
4mm to 1ft, 1:76 scale
18.83mm gauge (inside track width)
As EM is still slightly underscale, P4, also known as Protofour and Scalefour) has been established, with a track gauge of 18.83mm. P4 is also a set of standards applicable to track, wheels and other fine scale aspects, and as a scale/ gauge ratio is exactly right – small wonder it has attracted those modellers that like to get closer to the prototype.

Several locomotive and rolling stock kit suppliers offer the option of a chassis or underframe plus wheel sets to fit this gauge. The wheels are finer scale – narrower, with shallower flanges, and it is generally accepted that full springing or compensation is essential in order to achieve trouble-free running. The Scalefour Society offers support and components.

Easy to assemble trackwork and/or ready-made track and pointwork are now available from one or two suppliers. Quite a lot of extra work is needed, but for those who want their 4mm scale models to have that 'slightly more realistic feel', it is well worth the effort.

HO Gauge
3.5mm to 1ft, 1:87 scale,
16.5mm gauge (inside track width)
This is the major system in the rest of the world and at 3.5mm to 1ft scale, the track gauge width at 16.5mm is virtually exact to scale for the standard gauge. HO and 00 must not be confused in any way, as the scale of HO is 0.5mm per ft (ie almost 15%) smaller. Although one can run HO rolling stock on 00 layouts, due to the track gauge being the same, the difference in scale means that the HO models, being undersize, will look wrong.

HO gauge is used for Continental European, American and Canadian models but *not* for British steam or diesel prototypes. A wide selection of models are manufactured although there are fewer kits and accessories to be found. Their availability in Britain is limited to a relatively small number of specialist suppliers, many of whom import directly from the overseas manufacturer.

Despite this there is sufficient following for overseas prototypes in Britain to support two magazines, *Continental Modeller* and *International Model Trains*. For the North American prototypes, the main US magazine is *Model Railroader,* which is also obtainable from a few specialist outlets.

TT gauge
3mm to 1ft, 1:101.6 scale
12mm gauge (inside track width)
This 'Table Top' gauge originated in the USA, and was produced at 2.5mm to 1ft, 1/120th scale, the same as some later East German models.

In 1957 Tri-ang introduced a range of ready-to-run models and accessories in a version of TT, scaled at 3mm to 1ft and marketed as TT3. A range of wagon kits from Peco and flexible track from GEM followed but support waned when N gauge became more popular in the 1960s. The models were of standard gauge prototypes, which meant that the track was almost 17.5% under scale.

Most of the present-day support is via the Three Millimetre Society, membership of which is essential if you expect to make any significant progress in this scale.

N Gauge
2mm to 1ft, but 1:148 scale in UK
9mm gauge (inside track width)
N gauge is roughly half the linear size of 00 and for any given size of baseboard you should in theory get four times as much track.

In practice you are unlikely to get three times as much, since you should take advantage of the smaller size to have longer trains, a proper scale station with wider platforms and siding access. It also allows the modeller to put the railway within a proportionally larger landscape, in the interests of greater realism.

The scale generally used for the commercially produced British N gauge models is 1/148th – which at 2mm to 1ft should more correctly be 1/152nd (see 2mm scale modelling later). In practice the difference between 1:148 and 1:152 is very small, and although British N gauge translates into an over-size error of 2.7mm in every 100mm in any model, it is accepted by all those who purchase commercially produced N Gauge, as is the use of any model buildings constructed to the accepted architectural scale of 1/150th.

A full range of track and points from Peco, a vast range of locomotives, rolling stock and accessories from the main ready-to-run manufacturer Graham Farish, together with a range of buildings from Ratio, provides virtually everything needed for a modern image British layout, as well as many steam outline locomotives.

Although the overall selection is still not as large as that available in 00, the range is increasing, and this gauge/scale combination has seen a marked gain in popularity in recent years.

In Europe and North America a scale of 1/160th is employed for N gauge models, running on 9mm gauge track.

2mm scale
2mm to 1ft, 1:152.3 scale
9.42mm gauge (inside track width)
Although 2mm scale models first appeared in the 1930s, the 2mm Scale Association, formed in 1960 (several years before the commercial slightly out of scale N Gauge made an appearance),

brought together those interested in building fine exact scale models. The 2mm Scale Association provides a range of handbooks and a magazine for members, it also offers various services for the scratch-builder, including a wheel profiling service and a number of rolling stock kits. This is not a scale for the feint-hearted, as a lot of work will be necessary. Whilst the wheels can be re-profiled on proprietary N gauge models, precise scale locomotives and rolling stock have to be scratch-built. Membership of the 2mm Scale Society is recommended.

Z Gauge
1.5mm to 1ft, 1:200 scale
6.5mm gauge (inside track width)
In so far as Z gauge is manufactured by the oldest firm in the business, Märklin, it is a commercial gauge, though the range is restricted to a few Continental models and an even smaller selection of US prototypes. It is quite expensive and it only has a small following in Britain.

NARROW GAUGE

Whereas any railway system with a track gauge greater than 'the standard gauge' of 4ft 8½in is defined as 'Broad Gauge', Narrow Gauge is any railway with a track gauge *less* than the standard gauge. In the prototype, the latter includes the extensive 3ft 6in systems in Japan and New Zealand and the 1-metre system used in Switzerland; also the many 3ft gauge railroads found in many countries – not least America and Ireland – plus many lesser gauges, used widely for feeder lines, mineral railways and industrial networks.

This aspect of modelling has many devotees, probably because of the large and varied choice of gauges and styles of railway. It is possible to devise one's own scale/gauge combination, as by careful selection of a prototype one can marry an established scale to an established gauge. A selection of the more popular scale/ gauge combinations follow:

G gauge
Scaled to suite modelled prototype
45mm gauge (inside track width)
This is essentially a garden or theme pub gauge, with models for 2ft, 2ft 3in, 3ft and metre gauge prototypes being available from specialist suppliers the more finely detailed models from LGB and Bachmann in the main, and the more toylike products from Playmobile. Although the individual items appear costly, they are cheaper than most Gauge 1 models. Peco also manufacture trackwork for this gauge.

Top: **TT gauge, scale 3mm to 1ft: 'Yeominster' is a fine example of what can be achieved in the scale by a model-maker prepared to make much of the layout for himself, aided by a limited range of kits and a good supply of essential components, mainly provided by the 3mm Scale Society.**

Centre: **00 in the garden – Daventry Garden Railway.** Photograph by Tony Wright

Bottom: **Narrow gauge modelling has a strong following, this example being a 009 (4mm scale on 9mm gauge) 'Glastreath' by Charles Inley.** Photograph by Tony Wright

SM32
16mm to 1ft scale
32mm (0) gauge track
Designed for large models of 2ft gauge prototypes,it is mainly the province of scratch-builders.
It is very popular with live-steam modellers since
the models are large enough to allow proper
engineering techniques to be applied. Peco also
make a special track for this system.

0 -16.5 Gauge
7mm to 1ft, 1:43.5 scale
16.5mm gauge (inside track width)
The use of what is essentially 00 gauge track
makes this suitable for modelling rolling stock
that would be found on a 2ft 3in or 2ft 6in full size
system. It is entirely a kit-based system.

00n3
4mm to 1ft, 1:76 scale
12mm gauge (inside track width)
This scale/gauge combination (00 scale, n for
narrow gauge, 3 for 3ft) is used for models of the
Isle of Man railways and the Irish 3ft gauge systems. It is growing in popularity, with an increasing selection of kits.

HOm
3.5mm to 1ft, 1:87 scale
12mm gauge (inside track width)
Although not quite to scale (11.5mm inside track
gauge would be more correct) this scale/gauge
combination is used for models of the Swiss
metre-gauge, and although quite costly, is gaining popularity largely because there is a now an
extensive selection of ready-to-run models, particularly of the Rhätian Railway – now said to be
the best supported prototype in the world. 'Avon'
could form the basis of an exciting metre gauge
layout.

HOn3
3.5mm to 1ft, 1:87 scale
10.5mm gauge (inside track width)
Very popular in the USA for modelling 3ft gauge
prototypes. The models are fairly expensive and
only available from a few specialist model shops.

009 / HOe or HO-9
4mm to 1ft, 1:76 scale
9mm gauge (inside track width)
There is no real difference between these two
sizes, which allow N gauge 9mm track chassis to
be used. In Britain 00-9 is well supported by small
specialist kit manufacturers and the 009 Society.

CLUBS & SOCIETIES
The moment you think seriously of adopting anything other than 00, HO or N, your first step
should be to join the appropriate specialist society and study their literature. Since you will often
be thrown onto your own resources, it is vital that
you know what the full wheel and track standards
are so that your models conform. Even more to
the point, it will be helpful, at least in the initial
stages, to have an experienced worker guide you
through some of the trickier parts and to know
where to go for help when you get stuck. Specialist societies also exist for the study of different
prototypes. Like the scale groups, they normally
publish regular journals or newsletters, in most
cases this alone is worth the membership fee.

Should you join your local model railway club?
Certainly, most club members agree that they
learned more about the hobby in their first month
than they found out in the previous year, but this
will only happen if you are able to take a full part in
club activities. So, unless the club meets at a time
and place convenient to you, there's little point in
paying the subscription unless the club is one of
the handful that publish a magazine or newsletter
which includes practical modelling features. Not
many do.

Most British clubs have as their core activity the
annual exhibition. This is a good place to find out
whether your local group is to your liking. Should
you want to exhibit your own layout, then membership of a club is a virtual necessity. Many people join at the exhibition, but a better arrangement
is to join just before the show and volunteer for
whatever job is going. This is the quickest and
most pleasant way of getting accepted in a society. It also brings home to you that you are only
going to get something out of your membership if
you are prepared to put something more than
your subscription into the club.

The most important thing to remember is that,
as with every hobby, you are building and operating a model railway so that you can spend your
spare time in an enjoyable fashion. Because
there are so many different railways to model and
so many different aspects of railway construction
and operation you can follow, you can find a combination that suits you. You don't have to conform
to anyone else's ideas or even model an actual
prototype. It's your railway, and you should build
and operate it as you think fit.

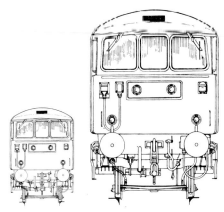

A BR Class 86 electric locomotive is illustrated
here, actual model size, in four of the most
popular scales used by railway modellers.

2mm scale   4mm scale   7mm scale   10mm scale, Gauge 1